WORKMAN PUBLISHING, NEW YORK

Design by Orlando Adiao

Library of Congress Cataloging-in-Publication Data is available.

ISBN 978-0-7611-4365-9

Workman books are available at special discount
when purchased in bulk for premiums and sales promotions
as well as for fund-raising or educational use.
Special editions or book excerpts also can be created to specification.
For details, contact the Special Sales Director at the address below,
or send an email to specialmarkets@workman.com.

Workman Publishing Company, Inc.
225 Varick Street
New York, NY 10014-4381
workman.com

WORKMAN is a registered trademark of Workman Publishing Co., Inc.

Printed in the United States of America

First Printing October 2006
18 17 16 15

Of Course
We're Kidding...

These "Would You Rather" choices aren't real ... but
they are fun to think and talk about. So, get ready for
the funniest, weirdest, and most mind-bending set of
questions and funky cool information that you can
imagine.

That's right: All the amazing questions in this book ask
you to decide between two choices—often grosser-than-
gross options from which you must positively choose.

Would You Rather ...
have to eat 50 peach pits
—OR—
all the seeds from 50 watermelons?

Gross, huh? But even though nobody would be dumb
enough to eat that stuff ... you still have to pick one.

So make your choice and then use your imagination and convince everyone to see where you are coming from . . . and laugh, giggle, and have fun the whole time. That's the purpose of *You Gotta Be Kidding!*—to get you, your friends, your parents, your grandparents . . . anyone and everyone . . . thinking, laughing, reasoning, and having a blast making goofy decisions. Each question also comes with the coolest, weirdest, most amazing info that you have ever heard. Definitely, the kind of stuff you will want to share with all your friends so they can see how smart and entertaining you are.

The *You Gotta Be Kidding!* rules:

1. **You must choose!** The phrases "I won't choose either," "Neither one," and/or "Who cares?" should never be heard while reading *You Gotta Be Kidding!* You must make a choice no matter how bad the options may be.

2. **Take it wherever you go.** The "Would You Rather" questions in this book are fun no matter where you are, but they're especially great to talk about on vacations and car trips. Take this book with you and have fun laughing and explaining to your friends and family why you make the goofy choices that you make.

3. **Use common sense:** Remember, these questions are obviously not real, so don't take any of them seriously. Everyone should know that trying to do or act out any of the questions in this book would be

really dumb and might cause you to get hurt or sick. **DON'T DO ANY OF THEM!** These questions are fun to talk about but dumb to do.

**OK then . . . Ready?
Ask someone the first question
and shake your head as they say,
"You Gotta Be Kidding!"**

WOULD YOU RATHER...

EAT A HAIR SANDWICH

OR

AN EARWAX OMELET?

- Human hair is about 91 percent keratin, which is a kind of protein. Sounds like that might be good for you, but the problem is, human stomachs can't digest hair.

- There's a reason earwax is so sticky: It helps trap dirt and kill bacteria and even small bugs that crawl into your ears. Those sure don't sound like things you want in an omelet!

WOULD YOU RATHER...

Have a fly frozen in every ice cube you put in your cold drinks

OR

Drink all your beverages from an unwashed tuna fish can?

Most bugs are actually pretty nutritious because, like most meat, they are full of protein. But, remember, flies eat all kinds of nasty things. So the little guy that's in your ice cube could've been eating dog poop an hour ago, which doesn't sound so good for you!

NOT BE ABLE TO EAT AGAIN UNTIL YOU SEE A BALD EAGLE IN THE WILD

OR

UNTIL YOU CAN FIND A FOUR-LEAF CLOVER?

It is believed that there are only about 100,000 bald eagles on the planet, and about half of them live in Alaska.

Finding a four-leaf clover is considered good luck, but they're not too easy to find. There are about 10,000 three-leaf clovers for every four-leaf clover.

WOULD YOU RATHER...

ALWAYS HAVE TO WRITE WITH YOUR "WRONG" HAND

ALWAYS HAVE TO WRITE WITH YOUR EYES CLOSED?

Around 10 percent of the population is left-handed. People who can use both hands equally well are ambidextrous. True ambidexterity is rare.

U.S. President James A. Garfield was ambidextrous. He sometimes entertained people by writing Greek with one hand and Latin with the other!

Drink a glass of really **OR** spicy mustard

Eat a bag of french fries found in a sidewalk garbage can?

Mustard is made spicy by adding horseradish, a root known for its zing. Humans have used it for more than 3,000 years and, for a long time, it was given as a medicine to treat pain. Horseradish is related to such delicious vegetables as cauliflower and Brussels sprouts.

WOULD YOU RATHER...

Be a boy and have a girl's name OR **Be a girl and have 10 brothers?**

Top Ten Girl's Names for 2005

1. Emily
2. Emma
3. Madison
4. Abigail
5. Olivia
6. Isabella
7. Hannah
8. Samantha
9. Ava
10. Ashley

"I grew up with six brothers.
That's how I learned
to dance—waiting for
the bathroom."
—Bob Hope

6

Be hit by OR Be bitten by lightning a shark?

A bolt of lightning can be as hot as 50,000 degrees Fahrenheit. That's about five times hotter than the surface of the sun!

An average of 16 shark attacks happen in the United States every year, but most of them aren't deadly.

Have hair so greasy it always drips, no matter how much you wash it

OR

Have a constant drooling problem?

We all have glands in our scalp that produce something called sebum—an oil that is nature's way of keeping our hair healthy. It's when those glands become overactive that you end up with really greasy hair.

GO TO YOUR FIRST DAY OF SCHOOL WITH YOUR EYEBROWS COMPLETELY SHAVED OFF

OR

WITH YOUR BOTTOM LIP PUFFED UP TO FIVE TIMES ITS NORMAL SIZE?

Mona Lisa (the woman in the famous painting by Leonardo da Vinci) has a very well-known face, but did you ever notice that she doesn't have any eyebrows?

Think about all the things it would be hard to do with a huge lip: eating, drinking, talking. . . .

WOULD YOU RATHER...

EAT A LiVE SNAKE

OR

A DEAD JELLYFiSH?

- Some people in China eat snake meat. It's supposed to be both delicious and good for your health. The Chinese have also been known to drink snake blood!

- Jellyfish are made up of 95 percent water.

WOULD YOU RATHER...

Wear a bicycle helmet everywhere you go

OR

Carry an open umbrella everywhere you go?

It's a common superstition that opening an umbrella indoors is dangerous—because if you do it, bad luck might *rain* down on you!

11

Never be able to cut your fingernails

OR

Never be able to cut your toenails?

The middle finger's nail grows the fastest.

Since 1991, the world record for longest toenails has been held by **Louise Hollis**. Her nails are each about 6 inches long.

SUCK A LITTLE OF THE DROOL OFF A DOG'S MOUTH AFTER HE COMES BACK FROM A RUN

OR

SHARE A BOWL OF DOG FOOD WITH A DOG AT THE SAME TIME HE'S EATING?

Many people believe that a dog's mouth is cleaner than a human's, but that all depends on what the dog has been putting in his mouth!

Always have a thick white **OR** coating of spit on your tongue

Always have really sweaty palms?

Even though spit is gross, there are good things about it too. It helps keep your mouth clean, makes it easier to swallow food, helps your tongue to taste, and helps digestion by starting to break down food while it's still in your mouth.

WOULD YOU RATHER...

NOT BE ABLE TO SEE

OR

BE ABLE TO SEE JUST FINE BUT NOT BE ABLE TO SMELL?

There are about 1.3 million legally blind people in the United States.

Most of our ability to taste things comes from being able to smell them, so, without the sense of smell, we also wouldn't be able to taste anything!

WOULD YOU RATHER...

HAVE ONLY NINE FINGERS

OR

ONLY TWO TOES?

- Toes may seem kind of useless, but they're actually very important because they help you keep your balance.

- Frodo Baggins, a character in *The Lord of the Rings,* had one finger bitten off by Gollum. That's why he's known as "Frodo of the Nine Fingers."

Spread nose pickings **OR** Spread the skin from a bunch of popped blisters over your cereal over your pizza?

There's actually an official medical term for eating boogers: mucophagy. Eating snot isn't always a good idea because it can have lots of nasty things in it—like dust and bacteria—that could make you sick.

Have a 20-pound seagull **or** poop on your head

Have a camel spit all over you?

In the 19th century, seagull poop was considered very valuable and was a popular fertilizer among farmers in the eastern United States and Great Britain.

Camel "spit" is actually a nasty stream of stomach juices, not just plain saliva like human spit.

WOULD YOU RATHER...

BE FORCED TO RUN ON A GIANT HAMSTER WHEEL AT SCHOOL EVERY DAY FOR AN HOUR

OR

BE FORCED TO ALWAYS DRINK ONLY FROM A BABY BOTTLE?

One company actually makes hamster wheels that are big enough for kids to run in. Maybe you'll get one for your next birthday!

Quenching your thirst would be really hard if you could drink only out of a baby bottle. It'd be like drinking a huge glass of water through a *really* tiny straw.

BE THE FIRST PERSON TO LAND ON MARS

OR

BE THE FIRST PERSON TO LIVE ON THE MOON?

It is estimated that the distance between Earth and Mars is 48 million miles. That means it would take around 260 days to get there. The atmosphere also isn't very friendly to humans: It's really, really, really cold (the average temperature is -81 degrees Fahrenheit!), and we aren't able to breathe the air.

Eat the first dead fish you find on the beach

OR

Eat a live 3-inch-long frog?

Ever wonder why dead fish are so stinky? Fish tissue contains a chemical called trimethylamine oxide, which doesn't smell when the fish is alive. But once the fish dies, this chemical breaks down into two kinds of ammonia, which produce that awful smell.

WOULD YOU RATHER...

Have your birthday on **OR** Have your birthday on Leap Day

Have your birthday on any other day of the year, but never be able to get any birthday presents?

If your birthday is on Leap Day (February 29), you'd have a birthday only during leap years, which happen only every four years.

There's a family in Norway who has three children who were all born on Leap Day!

WOULD YOU RATHER...

STAND STILL AT THE END
OF A TENNIS COURT WHILE THE
WORLD'S BEST TENNIS PLAYER
RIPS 100 BALLS IN A ROW AT YOU

STAND STILL ON HOME PLATE AND
LET A MAJOR LEAGUE PITCHER THROW
20 BASEBALLS AT YOU?

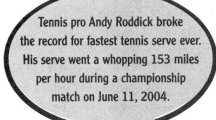

Tennis pro Andy Roddick broke
the record for fastest tennis serve ever.
His serve went a whopping 153 miles
per hour during a championship
match on June 11, 2004.

BE THE OLDEST OF FIVE SIBLINGS

OR

THE YOUNGEST OF FIVE SIBLINGS?

• The oldest child in a family often has to take on a lot of responsibility and help take care of younger siblings.

• The youngest children in a family are often "babied" and can feel frustrated because other people in their family don't treat them like grown-ups, even after they become adults.

Eat nothing but oatmeal topped with clumps of hair for a week

OR

Nothing but oatmeal that someone else has sneezed in?

Hair isn't digestible. If you eat too much hair, it builds up in your stomach and forms into big balls, which can block up your stomach and intestines. If you don't have the hairballs removed, they can eventually kill you.

Always have a lot of crust **OR** Always have green crust around your eyes

around your nostrils?

Eye goop is most common when you wake up in the morning. While you sleep, sweat, oil, and tears build up and, in the morning, you have a nice crust on your eyes.

KISS A MONKEY

KISS A WORM?

Even though adult monkeys are very cute, they can be really mean and often bite and pinch people.

Worms are slimy because they're coated in mucus. It may seem disgusting, but it's what allows them to breathe through their skin.

COME FACE-TO-FACE WITH A 10-FOOT-TALL PRAYING MANTIS

OR

WITH A 5-FOOT-TALL WEASEL?

Praying mantises usually bite the neck of their prey to paralyze it before they eat it alive.

Weasels are known for being fast and ferocious. They're not afraid to attack much larger animals, and they've been known to attack humans too. When attacked, weasels can produce a stink that is even smellier than a skunk's!

Drink liquid that's leaking **or** from a full garbage bag

Chew on a hairy clump found between the cushions of an old couch?

The smelliest substance on Earth is thought to be ethyl mercaptan, a chemical that smells as bad as rotting cabbage, garlic, onions, burnt toast, and sewer gas . . . all at once!

Try to run a 3-mile race without shoes and with a 1-pound flat rock tied to the bottom of each foot **OR** Run the same race while wearing a vest filled with 20 pounds of rocks?

A scientist in Australia found out that it's harder to run when extra weight is added on to your feet than when it's added around your middle. That's because when it's on your feet you have to lift it up and down when you run, which requires your body to use a lot more energy.

BE SOMEBODY'S PET CAT

OR

SOMEBODY'S PET DOG?

There are more than 58 million dogs in the United States. So, depending on which you choose, you'd have either lots of friends to play with or lots of bullies to deal with!

WOULD YOU RATHER...

Show up muddy and wet on your first day of school because you fell while running to try and make it there on time

OR

Risk being late to school because after you fell you went home to change?

Teacher: Why are you late to class?

Student: Because of a sign I saw on the road.

Teacher: What does a sign have to do with your being late?

Student: It said, SCHOOL AHEAD, GO SLOW!

EAT 10 POUNDS OF CHEESE IN ONE SITTING

OR

EAT A BUCKET OF PEANUT BUTTER WITH NOTHING TO DRINK?

It takes about 10 pounds of milk to make one pound of cheese, so eating 10 pounds of cheese is like drinking 100 pounds of milk!

It takes 850 peanuts just to make an 18-ounce jar of peanut butter. So imagine how many nuts you'd be eating if you ate a whole bucket of peanut butter!

WOULD YOU RATHER...

Sleep upside down like a bat OR Standing up like a cow?

Cows do sometimes take short naps while standing up, but when they're sleeping for real, they lie down on the ground.

Bats sleep hanging upside down because it puts them in a good position to take off into flight, and it's also a good way to hide from danger because few animals can reach the high places where bats hang.

Swim across a river that is filled with crocodiles **OR** **Spend the night on an island where man-eating tigers live?**

Supposedly, one way to escape the jaws of a crocodile is to jam your thumbs into its eyes until it lets go.

Tigers don't normally eat people, and they usually try to avoid us in the wild. But if a tiger is unable to hunt its normal prey, then it might go after a human that crosses its path.

WOULD YOU RATHER...

BE REALLY SMART BUT REALLY BORING

OR

REALLY DUMB BUT FUNNY AND ENTERTAINING?

- One study showed that boring people are seen as unintelligent and unfriendly, even if they're smart!

  - People who laugh a lot and have a good sense of humor are thought to be healthier and live longer.

WOULD YOU RATHER...

EAT FRIED MONKEY BRAINS

OR

EAT THE RAW GUTS FROM A HUGE SNAKE?

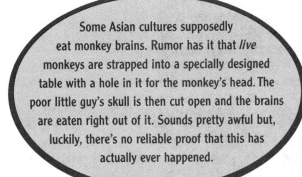

Some Asian cultures supposedly eat monkey brains. Rumor has it that *live* monkeys are strapped into a specially designed table with a hole in it for the monkey's head. The poor little guy's skull is then cut open and the brains are eaten right out of it. Sounds pretty awful but, luckily, there's no reliable proof that this has actually ever happened.

Be able to fly

OR

Be able to turn invisible?

One of the most common dreams people have is that they can fly. Kids have this dream more than adults do, and more than one third of people have dreamt that they can fly at some time during their life.

Nurse: Doctor, there is an invisible man in the waiting room.

Doctor: Tell him I can't see him now.

HAVE TO WEAR A BIG CLOWN NOSE FOR A MONTH

OR

A HUGE MEXICAN HAT FOR A MONTH?

The Mexican Hat Dance is so popular that it was made the official dance of Mexico. The dance starts by putting a sombrero (which means "hat" in Spanish) on the ground. Then, men dressed like cowboys and women wearing big, colorful skirts all twirl around the sombrero.

WOULD YOU RATHER...

BE CINDERELLA

THE FAIRY GODMOTHER?

Cinderella isn't the only one with a fairy godmother—they also show up in lots of other fairy tales. But no matter where they are, fairy godmothers all have one thing in common: magical powers that they use to help people.

Q: *Why is Cinderella bad at football?*
A: *Because she has a pumpkin as a coach.*

WOULD YOU RATHER...

Be on a picnic and find out that ants have crawled over all the food and silverware, but you still have to eat all the food

Find out that the apple you just bit into has a large worm inside and that you just swallowed a piece of it?

Ants are scavengers, and they're one of nature's best clean-up crews. Once an ant finds food, it lays a scent trail as it returns to the nest. That way, other ants can pick up this scent and follow the trail back to the food.

> Q: What's worse than finding a worm in the plump, juicy apple you just took a bite of?
>
> A: Finding only half a worm.

WOULD YOU RATHER...

GET TO SPEND THE DAY AT THE WHITE HOUSE WITH THE PRESIDENT

OR

AT THE HOUSE OF YOUR FAVORITE CELEBRITY?

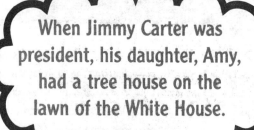

When Jimmy Carter was president, his daughter, Amy, had a tree house on the lawn of the White House.

Shave your head for a year OR Shave your eyebrows off for a year?

Common nicknames for people with shaved heads: Mr. Clean, Cue Ball, Smooth-Skull, and Bald by Choice.

Although eyebrows may seem small, each eyebrow has about 550 hairs in it.

WOULD YOU RATHER...

BE THE FASTEST RUNNER IN THE WORLD

THE FASTEST READER IN THE WORLD?

Jamaican sprinter Asafa Powell broke the world record for the fastest 100-meter run, which he ran in only 9.77 seconds on June 14, 2005, in Athens, Greece.

Howard Berg is the world's fastest reader. He can read more than 25,000 words per minute and write more than 100 words per minute!

44

WOULD YOU RATHER...

Drink 8 cups of month-old, dirty aquarium water

OR

Squeeze the dirty liquid from a gross, used sponge into your mouth?

Aquarium water is full of all kinds of nasty stuff like fish poop and scraps of uneaten fish food. That's gross enough, but when that stuff begins to rot, it releases ammonia, which is something you *really* don't want to be drinking!

BE ABLE TO TALK WITH ALL ANIMALS

OR

SPEAK ALL FOREIGN LANGUAGES?

- It's estimated that between 1.4 and 1.75 million animal and plant species have been discovered.

- More than 6,000 languages are spoken in the world.

Have eyeballs the size of golf balls

Have teeth the size of computer keys?

Humans normally have 32 permanent teeth in their mouths.

Computer keyboards usually have about 104 keys.

GO BACK IN TIME ONE MILLION YEARS

OR

GO INTO THE FUTURE ONE MILLION YEARS?

Humans didn't even exist
a million years ago. The earth
was experiencing an ice age and
much of the planet was covered
by huge glaciers.

Chew a piece of toenail off a man's dirty foot

OR

Lick every inch of his unwashed armpit?

Athlete's foot (a common fungus that grows on feet) can make toenails turn brown or yellow and get very thick. It can also cause smelly "toe jam" to build up under toenails.

Armpits stink because of germs growing there. Sweat by itself doesn't smell, but the germs feed on it and then produce waste—and it's the waste that smells so bad.

Be a soccer player and score a goal 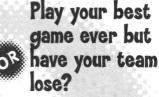 for the other team but still have your team win

Play your best game ever but have your team lose?

In soccer, when you score a goal for the team you're playing against, it's called an own goal. One poor guy, Staf Van Den Buys, scored three own goals in one match. Do you think he was voted Least Valuable Player on that team?

ALWAYS HAVE TONS OF COLD SORES IN YOUR MOUTH

OR

HAVE THE BACK OF ONE HAND ALWAYS FILLED WITH ITCHY, JUICY SORES?

Cold sores are really painful little blisters that usually show up on your lips, but you can also get them in your mouth or even on your nostrils, chin, or fingers. Once the blisters break they form a yellow crust.

WOULD YOU RATHER...

BEND DOWN TO PICK UP A PENCIL
AND HAVE YOUR PANTS SPLIT
IN FRONT OF YOUR ENTIRE CLASS

OR

REALIZE YOU'VE HAD
A "KICK ME" SIGN ON YOUR BACK
FOR THE ENTIRE DAY?

The KICK ME sign was
first used in Scotland for a
holiday called Taily Day,
which is like April Fool's Day
in the United States.

Let someone sneeze **or** directly into your open mouth

Have someone clean your ear with his tongue?

A sneeze can propel germs at speeds of up to 100 miles per hour.

Giraffes can clean their ears with their own tongues!

Try to take a banana from a giant monkey **OR** Try to take an egg from a mother goose while she's sitting on her nest?

Geese protect their eggs really well. Both the mother and father guard the nest, and if you try to steal an egg, you have two very angry geese to deal with!

WOULD YOU RATHER...

PAINT A LARGE WALL WITH A TOOTHBRUSH

OR

PAINT IT WITH A SPOON?

The first bristled toothbrush was made in China in 1498. They used bristles plucked from the backs of hog's necks and fastened them to bamboo or bone handles.

There are lots of types of spoons. Some are very common, like the teaspoon and soup spoon. And some are really bizarre, like the spoodle (a cross between a spoon and a ladle) or the ear spoon (used to remove earwax).

WOULD YOU RATHER...

HAVE TO DO FOUR HOURS OF HOMEWORK EVERY NIGHT

OR

ONE HOUR OF HOMEWORK EVERY NIGHT, BUT HAVE TO WRITE WITH A PEN TAPED TO YOUR NOSE?

Q: What's worse than having a pen with no ink?

A: Having two pens with no ink.

Eat a live moth with
a huge, gross body and
wings as big as your hand

OR

A dead hummingbird
including the feathers?

Most moths eat leaves
and flowers, and sometimes
they feed on mud and animal
dung to get the nutrients
they need.

Hummingbirds are the
smallest bird species in the world.
Their wings beat up to 78 times per
second, and they can fly all kinds of
ways—forward, backward, hovering,
and even upside down.

WOULD YOU RATHER...

WRITE "i AM AN iDiOT" 10,000 TiMES WiTHOUT STOPPiNG

OR

SUCK 75 THiCK MiLKSHAKES THROUGH A SKiNNY STRAW WiTHOUT RESTiNG?

Here's how to make a chocolate milkshake:

In a blender, put 2 cups of milk, 1 cup of vanilla ice cream, and a few tablespoons of chocolate syrup. Then blend until smooth. If you want the shake to be thicker, add more ice cream.

WOULD YOU RATHER...

Drink a small cup of pus from a huge blister

OR

Eat a salad covered with "Bits O' Scabs"?

The fluid inside a blister is also called serum, and it's actually sterile (that means there are no germs in it)—until the blister is popped.

Those crusty, dark, reddish brown things we call scabs are blood clots that have dried up. Even though it's tempting to pick scabs, you should try not to— scabs fall off by themselves when your wound is healed.

RIDE FOR ONE FULL DAY IN THE BACK OF A TRUCK THAT IS JAM-PACKED WITH COWS

DRIVE FOR THREE FULL DAYS IN A CAR WHILE SITTING ON A SEAT THAT HAS NO BACK?

Cows swallow huge amounts of air to help them digest food, and that makes them produce lots and lots of gas. The good news is that their farts aren't very stinky. The bad news is that the farts tend to be very noisy and can last for a *really* long time.

EAT A HUGE PLATE OF UNCOOKED, WET BROWN SEAWEED

OR

A LARGE CUP OF DRY, GRAINY SAND?

• There's a gum made from seaweed that's often used to thicken ice cream. So you're sort of eating seaweed whenever you're enjoying a delicious ice-cream cone. Yummy!

• Sand is basically a pile of very tiny rocks.

Be a stuntman and jump off a 100-foot cliff into the ocean wearing a blindfold

OR

Be a stuntman and jump off a 200-foot cliff but not be blindfolded?

Q: Why didn't the dime jump off the cliff after the nickel?

A: Because he had more cents!

62

BE CAUGHT IN A STORM WHILE IT'S RAINING ROCKS THE SIZE OF BASEBALLS

OR

WHILE IT'S RAINING DARTS?

In outer space it really does rain rocks! It's called a meteor shower. But the rocks there are a lot bigger than baseballs (they can be up to 30 feet wide)!

A raindrop falls about 600 feet per minute, and a snowflake falls about 11 feet per minute.

Get a really bad wedgie OR Get a really bad noogie?

An Atomic Wedgie,
the worst kind of wedgie, is when
the waistband of your underwear is
pulled above your head. If the front
(instead of the back) of the underwear
is pulled up, it's called a Melvin.
Whatever you call it,
it's bound to be painful!

HAVE TO EAT 50 PEACH PITS

OR

ALL THE SEEDS FROM 50 WATERMELONS?

Peach pits contain a chemical
that is poisonous to humans,
and so it's very dangerous to eat them.
Luckily, peach pits are very large
and hard to chew so most people
don't try to eat them.

WOULD YOU RATHER...

ONLY BE ABLE TO SEE THE COLOR GREEN AND SEE EVERYTHING ELSE IN SOME SHADE OF GRAY

SEE EVERYTHING SLIGHTLY OUT OF FOCUS?

Colorblind people sometimes have an advantage over other people. The military has found that colorblind soldiers can often spot something that is camouflaged, which nobody else can see.

Out-of-focus, or blurred, vision is sometimes caused by a serious eye problem, but the most common reason that people can't see clearly is because they need glasses!

WOULD YOU RATHER...

HAVE TO WIND UP GARDEN HOSES ALL DAY, EVERY DAY

OR

HAVE TO DIG HOLES FOR POSTS ALL DAY, EVERY DAY?

Q: If five people dig up a field in one day, how long will it take ten people to dig up the same field?

A: No time at all. The field has already been dug up!

Get to pitch the first inning for a OR **Play in the first quarter of an NBA basketball game?**

major league baseball team

At 15 years old, Joseph Henry Nuxhall was the youngest major league baseball player ever. He pitched a single game for the Cincinnati Reds in 1944 and then didn't play in the major leagues again until 1952.

Kobe Bryant is the youngest player ever to start in an NBA game. He was only about 18-and-a-half years old when he started for the Los Angeles Lakers.

Always have to wear 3-D glasses

OR

Always have a milk mustache?

You can make your own 3-D glasses. Just cut cardboard in the shape of glasses and then cut out space for your eyes to see through. Tape or glue red cellophane over the left eyehole and put blue cellophane over the right eyehole. Put on the glasses, and you're ready to see in 3-D!

WOULD YOU RATHER...

Have all your senses work only half as well as they do now

OR

Lose one sense altogether?

Most people think that humans have only five senses (sight, hearing, touch, smell, and taste). But scientists now agree that we have at least nine senses and maybe as many as 21, including the ability to feel heat and to feel pain.

WOULD YOU RATHER...

SPEND THE DAY SWIMMING WITH DOLPHINS

OR

TAKE A LONG RIDE ON AN ELEPHANT?

- Dolphins are known for being friendly toward humans. There are many tales of dolphins protecting shipwrecked sailors by swimming circles around their boat to keep sharks away.

- Elephants are the biggest land animals in the world. They can be aggressive, but throughout history they have been domesticated and used for transportation.

HAVE TO RUN ACROSS THE TOPS OF FIVE FAST-MOVING TRAIN CARS

HAVE TO SLOWLY CRAWL ALONG A 6-INCH LEDGE AROUND THE FIFTH FLOOR OF A BUILDING?

The fastest train in the world is the TGV (which stands for Train à Grande Vitesse) in France. It normally runs at 186 miles per hour, but it can reach a speed of 300 miles per hour (which is about half the speed of sound)!

WOULD YOU RATHER...

SUCK THE WHITE DRIED SPIT OFF THE EDGES OF A TEACHER'S LIPS AFTER A TWO-HOUR CLASS

SUCK OFF THE CRUD THAT GATHERS IN THE CORNER OF A CAT'S EYE?

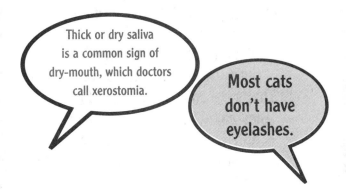

Thick or dry saliva is a common sign of dry-mouth, which doctors call xerostomia.

Most cats don't have eyelashes.

73

Have your skin change colors based on how you are feeling ... like red for anger or blue for sadness

OR

Have your skin change to the color of whatever you last ate ... like green for peas or purple for grape soda?

When you blush, the lining of your stomach becomes redder.

Flamingos are born white but turn pink as they grow. That's because a lot of the food they eat—like shrimp—has a nutrient in it that adds the color to their feathers.

GROW TUSKS
OR
GROW ANTLERS?

- Animals' tusks and teeth are a lot alike. Tusks are made of the same material as teeth—they're just bigger and in a different place.

  - Antlers are one of the fastest-growing animal tissues. Those huge antler racks that you see on deer and moose can grow in as little as three to four months.

Be able to walk on water any time you want

OR

Be able to fly for three hours at a time but for only three times in your life?

There are several small animals and insects that actually do walk on water, like the Jesus lizard and the fisher spider.

WOULD YOU RATHER...

EAT THE CHEWED FOOD OUT OF A STRANGER'S MOUTH

OR

CLEAN BETWEEN A STRANGER'S TOES WITH YOUR TONGUE?

Scientists have discovered that more than 500 types of bacteria live in a normal person's mouth.

In 16th-century France, it was traditional for a newly married couple to stand naked outdoors while the groom kissed the bride's left foot and big toe.

HAVE YOUR ONLY TOY BE AN ETCH A SKETCH

A CONTAINER OF SILLY PUTTY?

The Etch A Sketch was first marketed in 1960 and, since then, more than 100 million of them have been sold.

In space, things are always floating away because there's no gravity. The astronauts on *Apollo 8* found a good solution: They used Silly Putty to keep their tools in place!

Have to fish in a large pond until you catch something and be allowed to use only your bare hands

OR

Have to completely untangle a golf-ball-sized knot of thread?

It is difficult but not impossible to catch a fish with your bare hands. Any sudden movement will scare the fish away, so slowly sneak up on a fish. Once it's within your reach, place your hand under it and tickle its belly (this is no joke!). Tickling is supposed to make a fish sleepy, and then you'll be able to grab it and lift it out of the water.

Not be able
to recognize
anyone
else's face

OR

Be able to
see everyone
else's face
but never
your own
face?

There is a disorder called
prosopagnosia that makes
it really hard or even
impossible for a person to
recognize other people by
their faces. In severe cases
a person may not even be
able to identify his own face
in a mirror.

DRINK A GLASS OF YOUR OWN DAY-OLD SPIT

A GLASS OF SOMEONE ELSE'S OWN SWEAT?

The average person makes 10,000 gallons of saliva during his life.

The average person has more than 2 million sweat glands over her entire body. Even though we may not notice it, we're constantly sweating.

NEVER BE ABLE TO LISTEN TO YOUR FAVORITE SONG AGAIN

OR

NEVER BE ABLE TO WATCH YOUR FAVORITE TV SHOW AGAIN?

Q: What's an Eskimo's favorite song?

A: "Freeze a Jolly Good Fellow!"

WOULD YOU RATHER...

Discover space aliens that are smarter than we are  That are dumber than we are?

Q: What's an alien's favorite dessert?
A: Martian-mallows.

More than half of all reported (though not necessarily real) alien sightings occur between the hours of 7 P.M. and midnight.

83

HAVE TO READ EVERY BOOK STARTING FROM THE BACK AND GOING TO THE FRONT

OR

READ EVERY BOOK WHILE HOLDING IT UPSIDE DOWN?

A palindrome is a word or phrase that reads the same way forward and backward. One example is this good advice: Step on no pets.

Some people who have difficulty reading find that turning a book upside down actually makes it easier for them to read!

WOULD YOU RATHER...

EAT AN ENTIRE WATERMELON INCLUDING THE SEEDS AND RIND

OR

DRINK A PITCHER FULL OF CORN DOG BATTER?

Some people think that eating watermelon seeds causes a watermelon to grow in your stomach, but that's not true. Watermelon seeds are perfectly safe to eat, and in some places baked watermelon seeds are a popular snack.

YOUR HEAD WAS TWICE ITS NORMAL SIZE

OR

HALF ITS NORMAL SIZE?

On average, an adult's head weighs about eight pounds.

There are companies that make hats to fit people with extra-large heads.

WOULD YOU RATHER...

Have a little man live in your mouth and hammer on your teeth with a pick all day

OR

Have a small bird live on your nose and yank out your nose hairs whenever it wants to?

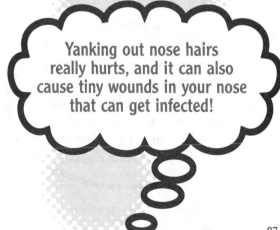

Yanking out nose hairs really hurts, and it can also cause tiny wounds in your nose that can get infected!

WOULD YOU RATHER...

BE ONSTAGE IN A SCHOOL PLAY AND SUDDENLY GET A NOSEBLEED

BE ONSTAGE AND GET A LOUD CASE OF THE HICCUPS?

Charles Osborne got the hiccups in 1922 and couldn't find any cure for them. He kept on hiccuping until one day in 1990 when they finally stopped. Those 68 years of constant hiccups earned him the Guinness World Record for Longest Attack of Hiccups!

Cut a baseball field of grass with your teeth

OR

Lick up a huge rain puddle?

Humans can't digest grass. If we eat it, it makes us sick.

Water in puddles has all kinds of nasty stuff in it—dirt, pollutants, germs, plant parts, and even bits of bugs!

WOULD YOU RATHER...

ALWAYS HAVE TO KEEP ONE HAND TOUCHING ANOTHER PERSON

OR

NEVER BE ABLE TO TOUCH ANOTHER HUMAN BEING AGAIN?

A study found that by shaking hands
you can spread more germs than are found
on any one of these really germy things:
money, a toilet seat, hotel bed sheets,
dogs, swimming pools, fish tanks,
pay phones, public restrooms,
kitchen sponges, or water fountains.

WOULD YOU RATHER...

Run half of a marathon running backward A full marathon running normally?

- Timothy Badyna ran an entire marathon running backward, and he finished it in the amazingly short time of 3 hours, 53 minutes, and 17 seconds.

- An official marathon is 26 miles and 385 yards long. It used to be exactly 26 miles, but at the 1908 Olympics in London, England, an extra 385 yards were added to put the finish line in front of the royal box so the royal family would have a better view. And the mileage has remained the same ever since.

BE STUCK IN A TINY ROOM ALL NIGHT WITH YOUR DAD WHILE HE IS SOUND ASLEEP AND SNORING AS LOUD AS A MOTORCYCLE

OR

BE STUCK IN THE SAME ROOM ALL DAY WITH A HUGE PILE OF YOUR WHOLE FAMILY'S DIRTIEST SOCKS?

You can sometimes stop people from snoring by making them sleep on their side instead of their back.

Air conditioners can develop something called Dirty Socks Syndrome, which occurs when germs grow inside them and cause them to smell like—you guessed it—dirty socks!

WOULD YOU RATHER...

LICK ALL THE MAKEUP OFF A CLOWN'S FACE

LICK YOUR REFRIGERATOR CLEAN WITH YOUR TONGUE?

Recipe for Clown Makeup

2 teaspoons vegetable shortening
5 teaspoons cornstarch
1 teaspoon white all-purpose flour
3 or 4 drops of glycerin
Food coloring, if desired

Use a rubber spatula to blend the first three ingredients until a smooth paste is formed. If you want a creamier consistency, add the glycerin. To remove the makeup, use shortening or baby oil.

WOULD YOU RATHER...

LICK SOMEONE'S EYEBALL

OR

HAVE YOUR EYEBALLS LICKED BY SOMEONE ELSE?

Some reptiles, like geckos,
clean their eyeballs
by licking them.

WOULD YOU RATHER...

HAVE TO GO OFF AN OLYMPIC-SIZE SKI JUMP ON YOUR BICYCLE

ON YOUR ROLLERBLADES?

An Olympic ski jump is around 295 feet high.

WOULD YOU RATHER...

THAT YOUR PARENTS KISSED EACH OTHER... LONG AND SLOPPY... RIGHT IN FRONT OF A GROUP OF YOUR FRIENDS

THAT YOUR PARENTS TALKED REALLY LOVEY-DOVEY AND SAPPY FOR A WHILE IN FRONT OF YOUR FRIENDS?

Richard Langley and Louisa Almedovar set the Guinness World Record by kissing for 30 hours.

Lick a melted chocolate **or** Lick an old couch until it was totally clean . . . even in all the cracks?

bar off the sidewalk

A study showed that 52 percent of adults in the United States said chocolate is their favorite flavor. Vanilla and berry tied for second favorite flavor.

Dust mites are little bugs that live in fabric, like pillows and blankets, and feed on the tiny flakes of skin that constantly fall off people. Do you know where the most dust mites are usually found in a house? Right between the couch cushions.

97

WOULD YOU RATHER...

HAVE THE ABILITY TO TURN INVISIBLE BUT HAVE NO CONTROL OVER IT, SO IT TURNS ON AND OFF RANDOMLY

OR

BE ABLE TO BREATHE UNDER WATER FOR AN HOUR AT A TIME?

• Right now there's currently no way for a human to truly become invisible. But there are ways to hide yourself so that other people can't see you—like standing behind something taller and wider than you are (duh!), or dressing to match whatever you're standing in front of so you'll be camouflaged.

• Beavers can hold their breath under water for 45 minutes at a time.

WOULD YOU RATHER...

BE STUCK FOR 24 HOURS AT THE TOP OF A STOPPED FERRIS WHEEL

BE STUCK HANGING UPSIDE DOWN ON A ROLLER COASTER FOR TWO HOURS STRAIGHT?

The Sky Dream Fukuoka in Japan
is the largest Ferris wheel in the world.
It's 367.45 feet in diameter
and 393.7 feet tall.

The Giant Drop in Australia
is the world's tallest free-fall roller coaster.
It drops almost 400 feet, which is
the height of a 39-story building.

Have to stay back one year in school

OR

Have no summer vacation for four years in a row?

Some schools in the United States have given up long summer vacations and switched to year-round schooling. But it's not so bad: The kids still get a summer break (although it's much shorter than a normal summer vacation) and other short vacations throughout the year.

BURN YOUR MOUTH REALLY BADLY EVERY TIME YOU EAT PIZZA

NEVER EAT PIZZA AGAIN?

In the United States 350 slices of pizza are eaten every second, which means each person is eating about 23 pounds of pizza per year!

There's a special term for when you've burned your mouth on hot pizza: pizza palate. Luckily pizza palate is usually minor and heals on its own after a few days.

WOULD YOU RATHER...

EAT A PEANUT-BUTTER-AND-JELLY SANDWICH MADE FROM A TUB OF PEANUT BUTTER THAT A BIG, SWEATY GROWN-UP JUST WALKED BAREFOOT THROUGH

OR

EAT A BOWL OF ICE CREAM THAT A WOMAN WITH BAD DANDRUFF JUST SHOOK HER HEAD OVER?

The average kid has eaten 1,500 peanut-butter-and-jelly sandwiches by the time he graduates from high school.

Did you know that each day a person inhales about 700,000 flakes of her own skin!

Have the power of Superman for one day per year The power of the president of the United States every day for a year?

Since Superman first appeared in a 1938 comic book, his powers have increased greatly. For example, he was first reported to be strong enough to lift a car with one hand, but 20 years later, he was able to hurl a planet through space and cause little earthquakes by clapping his hands.

WOULD YOU RATHER...

GET OUT OF THE BATHTUB ON A FREEZING MORNING AND DISCOVER THAT THERE'S NOTHING BUT A SMALL, DAMP WASHCLOTH TO DRY OFF WITH

FIND NOTHING BUT A BOX OF TISSUES TO DRY OFF WITH?

Most washcloths are made out of terry cloth, a fabric that's super absorbent.

Q: How do you make a tissue dance?

A: Put a little boogie in it!

LIVE IN A GIANT PINE TREE IN THE MIDDLE OF A HUGE FOREST

OR

IN A SMALL CAVE ON THE SIDE OF A MOUNTAIN?

- Pinecones can help you forecast the weather. Their scales will close up when it's about to start raining.

- Exploring a cave is called spelunking.

HAVE TO PAINT ALL THE WALLS AND THE CEILING OF A LARGE ROOM USING ONLY YOUR TONGUE

OR

PAINT THAT ROOM USING ONLY THE POINTED END OF A TOOTHPICK?

Paint usually has a lot of chemicals in it, some of which could be dangerous, so you *really* don't want to be putting it on your tongue.

WOULD YOU RATHER...

Walk knee-deep through fish guts

OR

Walk through a dark cave full of thick spiderwebs?

If fish guts are left lying around, maggots hatch and infest by the thousands—and eventually flies are swarming everywhere!

Spiderwebs are meant to be sticky so they can catch things. But they can get dirty quickly and can be ripped or pulled down easily. So, most spiders build new webs every day. What happens to the old webs? Spiders roll them into balls and eat them!

ALWAYS HAVE FiNGERNAiL FUNGUS

OR

ALWAYS HAVE NASTY NOSE WARTS?

- Nail fungus causes your nails to become thick and easily broken. It also makes them turn funny colors—and sometimes they even start to stink.

  - Warts usually go away on their own, but that can take months . . . or even years!

WOULD YOU RATHER...

HAVE NO TEETH AND TRY TO EAT A BiG BOWL OF CARAMEL POPCORN

TRY TO EAT FOUR BAGELS?

Owls don't have any teeth, so they swallow their prey whole. Then, after 12 hours or so, they cough up the parts they couldn't digest—like feathers, bones, and fur—and it comes out as a football-shaped pellet.

WOULD YOU RATHER...

Have to lick your desk at school until it is sparkling clean **or** Have to eat a whole box of crayons?

There are about 400 times more germs on an office desk than on a toilet.

Crayola comes from the French words for *oily* and *chalk*.

WOULD YOU RATHER...

Always have to stuff a soggy **OR** washcloth in your pants whenever you go out so that it looks like you wet your pants

Always have to wear a hat made out of a bird's nest?

There is a kind of straw hat that's called a Bird's Nest Hat, and—surprise, surprise—it looks a lot like a bird's nest!

TAKE A SHOWER EVERY DAY FOR ONE WEEK USING BABY POWDER INSTEAD OF WATER

OR

USING MOUTHWASH INSTEAD OF WATER?

Baby powder is sometimes used as a dry shampoo. You brush it into your hair and then brush it out and, along the way, it soaks up some of the grease in your hair.

Mouthwash actually works as a deodorant, because it helps kill the bacteria that cause body odor.

EAT
10 RAW POTATOES
OR
100 HOT PEPPERS?

Hot peppers have a chemical in them called capsaicin, which is what makes them hot. The more capsaicin they have, the more they burn your mouth and throat.

Raw potatoes are safe to eat, except for the green parts (which can be toxic). Be warned, though, potatoes can cause you to fart!

GO BACK TO AN UNKNOWN TIME

OR

GO FORWARD TO AN UNKNOWN TIME?

Most scientists believe that time travel
probably won't be done in a time machine.
Instead time travel would be done
through a black hole or a wormhole
(which may not even exist) that would transport
us instantly to a different point in time.

Have nose hair that grows one **OR** inch per hour

Have ears that feel like they are always spinning?

At that rate, in only one day, you would have nose hairs that are two feet long.

Dizziness is caused by your inner ears. There are liquid-filled tubes inside each ear and when you move, they tell your body what position it's in. When you spin around, the liquid sometimes keeps moving even after you stop, and tricks your body into thinking it's still spinning.

BE KNOWN AS A THIEF

OR

AS A LIAR?

There are sometimes physical clues that reveal a person is lying. One is that the liar will try not to look people in the eye. Another is that liars will sometimes touch their faces (especially near their mouths) to try to hide their mouths while they talk.

WOULD YOU RATHER...

EAT SNOT ON YOUR STEAK

OR

A WORM IN YOUR PASTA?

- Each day a person recycles about a quart of mucus (which is what snot is made of) by swallowing it.

- Scientists are doing experiments in which people eat a parasitic worm called a helminth. They think it could be a cure for serious stomach problems.

WOULD YOU RATHER...

Be hiking in the woods and accidentally **OR** disturb a sleeping bear

Be hiking and be spotted by a giant hungry hawk flying overhead?

In Alaska, it's legal to shoot bears, but it's illegal to wake one up to take its picture.

Most hawks have such good vision that they can spot a mouse from a mile away.

Have to always wear a hard hat no matter where you go

OR

Have to always wear glasses with little windshield wipers on them?

Edward W. Bullard first invented the hard hat in 1919 as a way to protect miners from head injuries.

Windshield wipers were invented by Mary Anderson in 1903.

WOULD YOU RATHER...

FART TWICE AS OFTEN AS MOST PEOPLE

BURP TWICE AS OFTEN AS MOST PEOPLE?

Some people think men fart more than women do, but it's not true.

A person usually burps at least 10 to 15 times during the day.

PUT LIVER JUICE ON EVERYTHING YOU EAT

OR

COW SPIT ON EVERYTHING YOU EAT?

Liver is one of the most hated foods in the United States.

Cows produce 200 times as much saliva as humans do!

HAVE REALLY YELLOW TEETH

OR

REALLY YELLOW EYES?

- Yellow teeth can be caused by drinking coffee or tea and by smoking or chewing tobacco. Ick!

- When the whites of your eyes turn yellow, it's usually a sign that something is wrong with your liver, and you should go to the doctor.

Not to be able to do anything to clean up in the morning except brush your teeth

OR

Be able to wash your whole body except not be allowed to brush your teeth?

Before World War II, most people in the United States didn't brush their teeth every day. During the war the U.S. Army made soldiers brush their teeth, and after they came home the habit caught on with everybody.

WOULD YOU RATHER...

Be the person in the circus
who stands still while
the knife thrower
throws knives at him

OR

Be the person who puts his head
in the lion's mouth?

David Adamovich, who goes by
the name The Great Throwdini,
holds the Guinness World Record
for Most Number of Knives
Thrown. In March 2006, he
threw 72 knives around a human
target in only one minute!

EAT
20 ORANGE PEELS
OR
20 BANANA PEELS?

- Orange peels might not taste great and they're hard to chew, but they're perfectly safe to eat.

- One supposed way get rid of a wart is to rub the inside of a banana peel over it every night for a week or two.

Not be able to sleep for OR eat for one week?

Not be able to eat for one week?

Randy Gardner holds the world record for the longest time with no sleep. In 1965 he stayed awake for 11 days straight.

Choosing to go without food for a time is called fasting. The first meal of the day *breaks* the overnight *fast*, which is where the word *breakfast* comes from.

ALWAYS WEAR SNOWSHOES

 OR

ALWAYS WEAR SCUBA FLIPPERS?

Snowshoe hares are a kind of rabbit, and get their name because their back feet are shaped like snowshoes, which helps them walk easily over deep snow.

When Benjamin Franklin was a boy, he made his own swimming flippers out of wood.

HAVE THE HiCCUPS FOR A WHOLE YEAR

OR

HOP AROUND ON ONE FOOT iNSTEAD OF WALKiNG FOR A WHOLE YEAR?

There's no proven cure for hiccups, but people believe that all kinds of crazy things can make hiccups stop—including swallowing three times while holding your breath, drinking vinegar, and drinking a glass of water with a spoon touching your temple.

WOULD YOU RATHER...

Eat a whole vacuum bag full of dirt **OR** Eat all the lint that has been collected from 10 clothes dryers in three months?

The medical term for eating dirt is geophagy.

Dryer lint is mostly fuzzy fibers from clothes, but it can also contain hair, dirt, and anything else that's on clothes when they go in the dryer.

WOULD YOU RATHER...

Always come in second in every contest you enter

OR

Come in dead last 9 out of 10 times, but always come in first every 10th try?

One really unlucky guy, John Bellavia, has entered more than 5,000 contests, but he's never won anything.

BE A BOY AND HAVE A GIRL'S NAME

OR

BE A BOY AND ALWAYS HAVE TO WEAR LIPSTICK?

Many people think the name Wendy was made up by the author of the book *Peter Pan* (by J. M. Barrie), but actually it was used before that. It might even have originally been a boy's name.

Did you know that most lipstick contains fish scales?

Be lost in space with plenty of food and water but very little

OR

chance of anyone rescuing you

Be stranded on a desert island with not enough food and water but with a good chance of being rescued?

In space, astronauts cannot cry like they do on Earth, because there is no gravity, so the tears can't flow down their faces!

Mount Desert Island is a real island off the coast of Maine, but it's not really deserted—it's a popular place to visit.

WOULD YOU RATHER...

EAT
10 LIVE CATERPILLARS
AS BIG AS YOUR THUMB
OR
FOUR DEAD TARANTULAS?

Caterpillars are a source of protein and have been eaten in Africa, Asia, Australia, and Latin America.

Shave off all the hair on your body including your eyebrows

OR

Dye all the hair on your body neon green?

It could take a while to do either of these things, since adults have more than 20 square feet of skin (about the size of a large blanket) and about 5 million hairs.

HAVE YOUR HEAD BE COMPLETELY FLAT ON TOP

OR

BE PERFECTLY ROUND LiKE A BASKETBALL?

Some people have their hair
cut into a flattop.
It's sort of like a crew cut,
but the hair on top sticks straight up
so the top of the head
appears totally flat.

135

WOULD YOU RATHER...

LOSE THE ABILITY TO BE AFRAID

LOSE THE ABILITY TO FEEL PAIN?

Fear can help warn your body of situations that could be scary or dangerous.

Even though it hurts, pain is important because it can help your body recognize that it is in danger and protect itself from serious injury.

HAVE TO SLEEP IN A BED WITH A CUP OF CRACKER CRUMBS AND A CUP OF SAND POURED ON THE SHEETS

OR

HAVE TO WALK AROUND ALL DAY, EVERY DAY, WITH GRAPE JELLY IN YOUR SHOES?

Did you know that the typical peanut-butter-and-jelly sandwich eaten at the beach contains more than 7,000 grains of sand?

Have everyone in the **OR** world other than you be an adult

Have everyone in the world be a kid?

The world's population is estimated to be over 6.5 billion people.

Around the world, 261 babies are born every minute.

138

GET POISON IVY ALL OVER YOUR REAR END

OR

BETWEEN ALL YOUR FINGERS AND TOES?

Here's a little rhyme
to help you remember to
avoid poison ivy:
*Leaves of three—
let them be!*

WOULD YOU RATHER...

BE STUCK IN AN ELEVATOR WITH SOMEONE WHO TALKS TOO MUCH

OR

WITH SOMEONE WHO WON'T TALK AT ALL?

In 1987 the record for longest time trapped in an elevator was accidentally set by a 76-year-old woman who got stuck for six days. Luckily, at the time, she was on her way home from the grocery store, so she had plenty to eat!

WOULD YOU RATHER...

SUCK PEA SOUP FROM AN OLD MAN'S BEARD

EAT THE DROOL OF A BABY WHILE SHE'S EATING STRAINED PEAS?

Janet Harris, of England, holds the world record for eating peas. In 1984 she ate 7,175 peas, one at a time, using chopsticks.

WOULD YOU RATHER...

Always wear a **OR** hairnet

Always wear giant floppy clown shoes?

Normally, people lose about 80 hairs every day.

Bet you didn't know that those clown shoes are among the most expensive parts of a clown's outfit.

HAVE
KNEES THE SIZE OF
WATERMELONS

ELBOWS AS LARGE
AS PUMPKINS?

In addition to the typical large watermelon, a much smaller type is grown that can fit easily in a refrigerator.

Large pumpkins (like the kind carved at Halloween) usually weigh between 20 and 80 pounds, but there are also many smaller varieties available.

143

GET THREE BEE STINGS IN ONE DAY

OR

HAVE MOSQUITOES BITE YOU FOR A WEEK?

Bees normally sting only when they are angry. So if one starts buzzing around you, don't swat at it. It really makes them mad and gives them a reason to sting you!

The best way to avoid mosquito bites is to wear long pants and long-sleeved shirts when you're going to be in a place with mosquitoes.

SWALLOW A TEASPOON OF SNAIL SLIME

OR

SWALLOW A TEASPOON OF COLD FISH EYES?

A company in South America makes cough syrup with snail slime in it because the slime is believed to have healing properties.

BE STRANDED IN THE MIDDLE OF THE DESERT WITH ONLY A SMALL BOTTLE OF WATER

WITH ONLY A BLACK UMBRELLA?

Without water to drink, most people will die within three to four days.

If you're out in the hot sun for a really long time, you can get sunstroke. That's when your body becomes overheated and can't cool itself down.

Run across the back Run underneath the legs of an angry elephant?

of a hungry alligator

The worst crocodile attack in history is believed to have been in 1945 when an Imperial Japanese Army unit was forced to cross 10 miles of swamp to meet up with another Japanese battalion. Thousands of saltwater crocodiles, each about 15 feet long, lived in the swamp and, by the end of the journey, only 20 out of the group of 1,000 Japanese soldiers had survived.

WOULD YOU RATHER...

SWALLOW A REALLY OLD PiECE OF ROCK-HARD GUM YOU FOUND STUCK TO THE BOTTOM OF A CAFETERiA TABLE

CHEW A HUNK OF GUM YOU FOUND THAT iS FRESH AND EVEN STiLL A LiTTLE WET?

- Dried chewing gum sticks so well to things that a power washer is usually needed to remove it.

  - Some people say that if you swallow gum it'll stay in your stomach for seven years. It is true that the body doesn't digest gum, but usually it passes through and comes out the way everything else does!

148

WOULD YOU RATHER...

HAVE TO EAT
100 HOT DOGS IN ONE HOUR

1,000 FRENCH FRIES
IN ONE HOUR?

In 2000 more than 20 billion hot dogs were eaten in the United States!

One out of every four potatoes consumed in England is eaten in the form of French fries.

HAVE
A PROSTHETIC ARM
iN THE PLACE OF
ONE OF YOUR REAL ARMS

A PROSTHETIC LEG
iN PLACE OF
ONE OF YOUR REAL LEGS?

Artificial limbs have been in use
for thousands of years—
some were even discovered
in a tomb in Italy
from 300 B.C.!

Have a birthday party without **OR** your best friend there

Have a party where no one shows up except your best friend?

"Friends are the bacon bits in the salad bowl of life."
—Anonymous

WOULD YOU RATHER...

FIND A HORNETS' NEST IN YOUR CLOSET

FIND A NEST OF RATTLESNAKES UNDER YOUR BEDROOM FLOOR?

A snake charmer once found 3,500 poisonous cobras beneath the floors of two houses in Bangladesh.

LICK A LARGE FROG ALL OVER ITS BODY

OR

EAT ONE BITE OF A PIECE OF ROTTEN FRUIT THAT'S FULL OF WORMS?

A goliath frog, which lives in West Africa, can grow to be up to a foot long. It usually weighs about as much as a cat and is the largest known type of frog.

WOULD YOU RATHER...

BE ON A TEAM
THAT LOSES MOST OF ITS GAMES
BUT IS KNOWN FOR PLAYING WELL
AND WITH A LOT OF HEART

ON A TEAM THAT
WINS ALL ITS GAMES EASILY,
BUT EVERYONE KNOWS THAT THE
PLAYERS DON'T TRY VERY HARD
OR EVEN CARE ABOUT THE GAME?

In 1916 Georgia Tech defeated
Cumberland College, 222 to 0—
the most one-sided football
game in history.

JUMP INTO A SWIMMING POOL FILLED WITH TONS OF ANTS

JUMP INTO A SWIMMING POOL FILLED WITH MILLIONS OF FLIES?

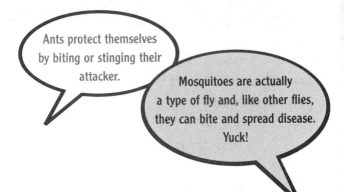

Ants protect themselves by biting or stinging their attacker.

Mosquitoes are actually a type of fly and, like other flies, they can bite and spread disease. Yuck!

WOULD YOU RATHER...

BE A TWIN

OR

BE AN ONLY CHILD?

- There are about 125 million multiples (that includes twins, triplets, etc.) in the world.

- Researchers have found that in terms of intelligence and achievement, if you are an only child you have a slight advantage over someone with a brother or sister.

Drink a gallon of seawater

OR

Drink a gallon of fresh toilet water?

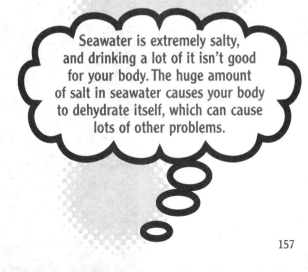

Seawater is extremely salty, and drinking a lot of it isn't good for your body. The huge amount of salt in seawater causes your body to dehydrate itself, which can cause lots of other problems.

Have a head full **OR** of lice

Be infected with ringworm?

Lice are very small parasites that attach to the hair on your head and feed off the oil and skin flakes from your head.

Ringworm isn't actually caused by a worm. It's a contagious fungal infection, which causes red, itchy patches that look like rings to show up on your skin.

WOULD YOU RATHER...

TRAVEL AROUND THE WORLD IN A HOT AIR BALLOON

TRAVEL AROUND THE WORLD IN A SAILBOAT?

Hot air balloons can be made in funny shapes—like hot dogs and rocket ships.

The smallest sailboat ever to sail all the way across the Atlantic Ocean was the 5-foot 11-inch *April Fool*. It was sailed by Hugo Vihlen in 1968, who made the trip in 84 days.

WOULD YOU RATHER...

BE A GIRL AND HAVE TO WEAR YOUR HAIR IN A MOHAWK FOR THE REST OF YOUR LIFE

BE A GIRL AND HAVE A BEARD FOR THE REST OF YOUR LIFE?

The average man spends about 145 days of his life shaving, which means not having a beard is a lot of work.

Some people use glue to keep their Mohawks standing up straight!

EAT A SMALL GARTER SNAKE

OR

EAT FIVE BIG SLUGS?

• Garter snakes eat worms, frogs, fish, and sometimes mice, but they aren't poisonous to humans.

• When attacked, slugs emit a thick coat of mucus and make their bodies shorter and fatter. This makes it harder to eat them and makes them taste bad to predators.

Have a
snowball fight
with a pro **OR** Play
baseball
pitcher

dodgeball
against
a pro
quarterback?

It's believed that
Mark Wohlers threw the
fastest pitch ever. It happened
during spring training in 1995
when he threw a pitch at
103 miles per hour.

Always have to carry dirty socks in **OR** your mouth wherever you go

Always have to use your tongue to flush The toilet?

The strongest muscle in the human body is the tongue.

WOULD YOU RATHER...

BE STUCK IN A DARK, WARM PLACE

OR

IN A COLD, LIGHT PLACE?

Fear of being in a dark place is called lygophobia.

Fear of light is called photophobia.

WOULD YOU RATHER...

EAT A COOKED BEAVER TAIL

OR

A COOKED COW UDDER?

There's a Canadian recipe for beaver-tail beans: The beaver's tail is cut off, cooked over a fire (to remove the skin), and then boiled in a pot of beans until it's tender. Sound delicious to you?

CLIMB TO THE TOP OF MOUNT EVEREST AND THEN LOSE YOUR HAT

LOSE YOUR GOGGLES?

Humans lose between 30 and 50 percent of their body heat through the head, so wearing a hat is a good way to stay warm.

WOULD YOU RATHER...

GO TO SLEEP ON A CAMPING TRIP
IN A TENT AND WAKE UP
WITH ANTS IN YOUR NOSE
AND EARS

WITH YOUR TENT MATE'S
TOE IN YOUR MOUTH?

Did you know that
there aren't any ants
in Iceland, Antarctica,
or Greenland?

Always have to sleep with one eye open

OR

Always breathe using only one lung?

There are some species of dolphin that sleep with one eye open.

The right lung takes in more air than the left lung does. That's because the left lung is smaller, so there's room for the heart.

EAT ONE CAN OF SOFT DOG FOOD

FIVE CUPS OF DRY DOG FOOD?

Dogs may love dog food, but most brands have some pretty nasty stuff in them, like the parts of meat that humans won't eat, including ground-up bones and sometimes even old grease from restaurants.

169

LICK 1,000 STAMPS

READ OUT LOUD FROM THE PHONE BOOK ALL THE LAST NAMES THAT START WITH A?

Diane Sheer holds
the world record for stamp licking.
She licked 225 of them
in five minutes.

GET A CAVITY FROM EATING TOO MUCH CANDY

OR

GET A HEADACHE FOR HALF AN HOUR EVERY TIME YOU EAT ICE CREAM?

You're more likely to get a cavity if you eat candy throughout the day rather than eating it all at once and brushing your teeth afterward.

Suck in some helium to hear yourself talk funny but have your voice stay like that

OR

Stick your teeth way out like a gopher and have them get stuck like that?

Helium is lighter than air, so it travels through your vocal cords differently than air does—that's why it ~~ a high, squeaky~~ ~~nakes you sound~~ ~~rtoon character.~~

171

WOULD YOU RATHER...

EAT POPCORN OFF THE FLOOR OF A MOVIE THEATER

EAT HALF OF A HAMBURGER THAT YOU PICKED OUT OF THE TRASH AT McDONALD'S?

The average person in the United States eats 54 quarts (that's about 130 cups) of popcorn each year.

McDonald's Big Mac is the world's bestselling burger.

Have your parents call you "Snookums" and "Cupcake" in front of all your friends

OR

Have to play a two-hour game of Twister with someone else's fat and sweaty grandma and grandpa?

The biggest Twister game ever was in 1987 at the University of Massachusetts at Amherst when 4,160 people played at once.

WOULD YOU RATHER...

Count all the grains of sand in a sand castle

OR

Count all the spoonfuls of water in a huge swimming pool?

The world's tallest sandcastle was built in 2003 by a bunch of people in Maine. The castle stood 29.25 feet high, and it took almost a month and 450 tons of sand to build it.

The world's biggest swimming pool is in Casablanca, Morocco. It is 1,574 feet long and 246 feet wide.

NEVER BE ABLE TO EAT OUT AT A RESTAURANT

OR

ALWAYS HAVE TO WALK EVERYWHERE?

Most families in the United States eat out three or more times a week.

In a lifetime, the average person will walk 74,670 miles, which is the same distance as three times around the world at the equator.

WOULD YOU RATHER...

EAT TWO MUD PIES MADE OF REAL MUD

OR

DRINK A CUP OF CAT SPIT?

People have been eating mud for thousands of years, and it *can* be good for your health (because mud contains a lot of important vitamins and minerals). But nowadays, because most dirt has all sorts of other nasty things in it—like chemicals—it's not a good idea to eat it.

WOULD YOU RATHER...

Wet your pants in front **OR** of your classmates

Be caught by your classmates while picking your nose and eating it?

Next time your friends catch you picking, tell them that one study shows that people who pick their noses (and eat it too) are healthier and happier. According to the study, picking keeps your nose cleaner, and eating what you pull out can strengthen your immune system.

WOULD YOU RATHER...

Leave a slime trail, like a snail, everywhere you walk **OR** Always leave a trail of smoke like an old car?

Snails produce their thick slime to help them move and to protect them as they go across rough surfaces. It also allows them to crawl hanging upside down.

WOULD YOU RATHER...

HAVE A THIRD EYE IN THE MIDDLE OF YOUR FOREHEAD

HAVE THREE ARMS?

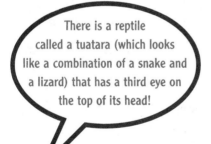

There is a reptile called a tuatara (which looks like a combination of a snake and a lizard) that has a third eye on the top of its head!

WOULD YOU RATHER...

EAT A HEAD OF ROTTEN LETTUCE

OR

DRINK A GLASS OF SOUR MILK?

Knock-knock.

Who's there?

Lettuce.

Lettuce who?

Lettuce in!

NEVER BE ALLOWED TO EAT CHOCOLATE AGAIN

OR

HAVE TO EAT CHOCOLATE AND NOTHING ELSE?

During the 16th and 17th centuries, eating chocolate was considered a sin.

People in the United States eat more than 2 billion pounds of chocolate each year.

WOULD YOU RATHER...

Never bathe **OR** Bathe only in the nearest river?

Many rivers, besides being full of fish poop and other natural pollutants, have sewage from nearby towns pumped into them.

SPEND THE DAY WITH YOUR FAVORITE ATHLETE

OR

WITH YOUR FAVORITE MOVIE STAR?

Soccer star David Beckham has a gigantic mansion in England, known as Beckingham Palace, which has an indoor swimming pool, a sound system that plays music in every room, and a recording studio. His kids have a huge playhouse with a drawbridge and a tree house that cost $40,000.

HAVE A JOB CLEANING SILVERWARE IN YOUR MOUTH

CLEANING GOLF BALLS IN YOUR MOUTH?

The White House has more than 13,092 knives, forks, and spoons.

Golf balls have between 330 and 500 dimples, which help the ball go farther and fly higher.

Always have rainbow-colored hair **OR** Always have braces on your teeth?

Most people who get braces have them on for about two years.

BE FORCED TO SHARE YOUR BEDROOM WITH AN ELEPHANT

OR

YOUR BATHROOM WITH A MAN WHO HAS WEIRD SKIN RASHES?

Elephants are the largest animals that live on land. They can weigh between 10,000 and 14,000 pounds, which is about as much as a school bus.

WOULD YOU RATHER...

BE EXTREMELY LUCKY **OR** BE EXTREMELY SMART ... BUT NOT BOTH LUCKY AND SMART?

Q: Why are fish so smart?

A: Because they live in schools.

WOULD YOU RATHER...

FIND OUT THAT THE PORK YOU JUST ATE WAS ACTUALLY HAMSTER MEAT

THAT THE RED BEANS IN THE CHILI YOU JUST ATE WERE ACTUALLY BEETLES?

Did you know that a certain type of beetle is ground up and used to give a bright red color to many of the foods you eat? Yep. Carmine, which colors everything from yogurt to candy, is made from the female cochineal beetle.

WOULD YOU RATHER...

Always wear earmuffs **OR** Always wear a nose plug?

In Central and South America it was once considered very fashionable for people to wear plugs in their earlobes, lips, and noses.

WOULD YOU RATHER...

Have to wear shoes that are **or** four sizes too big

Wear pants, without a belt, that are four sizes too big?

Think four shoe sizes bigger sounds like a lot? Matthew McGrory (the guy with the world's largest feet) wore size $29\frac{1}{2}$ shoes.

WOULD YOU RATHER...

HAVE TO USE A TOILET THAT IS REALLY, REALLY FILTHY AND GROSS

OR

GO TO THE BATHROOM WITH A STRANGER STANDING IN THE ROOM?

- A study shows that 55 percent of people in the United States would let someone else come in the bathroom while they use the toilet.

- The average toilet seat has 49 germs per square inch.

WOULD YOU RATHER...

DRINK THE DIRTY WATER FROM A FLOWER VASE

A CUP FULL OF THE LIQUID SQUEEZED FROM A SPONGE THAT WAS JUST USED TO CLEAN THE KITCHEN?

Because a sponge is full of tiny holes and usually moist, it's the perfect place for icky little bacteria to cozy up. That means that a used sponge is one of the germiest things around.

WOULD YOU RATHER...

SEE A GROUP OF BULLIES TORMENTING YOUR BEST FRIEND AND NOT BE ABLE TO DO ANYTHING ABOUT IT

OR

HAVE THEM TORMENT YOU, BUT NOT AS BADLY?

Q: How can you tell when bullies are lying?

A: You can hear them talking.

Sadly, bullying is a very common problem. Between 15 and 30 percent of all students have been bullied or have bullied someone else.

Be born with an elephant trunk

OR

A giraffe neck?

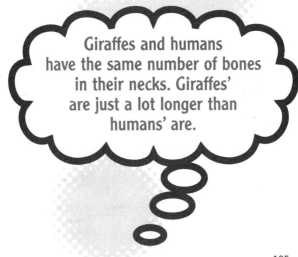

Giraffes and humans have the same number of bones in their necks. Giraffes' are just a lot longer than humans' are.

WOULD YOU RATHER...

LIVE IN A WORLD WHERE ALIENS ARE OUR MASTERS

WHERE INSECTS ARE OUR MASTERS?

Q:
What did the alien say to the book?

A:
"Take me to your reader!"

WOULD YOU RATHER...

Have a mouse run up your pant leg

OR

Have mosquitoes get caught inside your shirt?

Mice have very sharp teeth and are very good climbers.

Most mosquitoes have 47 teeth.

WOULD YOU RATHER...

Bang your funny bone five times in a row until it's not funny anymore

OR

Listen for 20 minutes to somebody scraping their nails down a chalkboard?

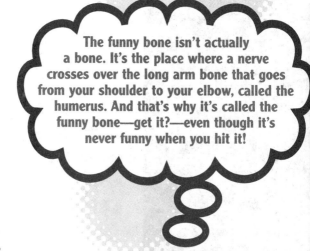

The funny bone isn't actually a bone. It's the place where a nerve crosses over the long arm bone that goes from your shoulder to your elbow, called the humerus. And that's why it's called the funny bone—get it?—even though it's never funny when you hit it!

WOULD YOU RATHER...

HAVE A PET COW THAT YOUR FAMILY GETS ALL *OR* **ITS MILK FROM**

HAVE A PET CHICKEN THAT LAYS ALL THE EGGS YOUR FAMILY USES?

Did you know that a cow normally makes almost 200,000 glasses of milk in its lifetime?

Most hens lay an average of 257 eggs a year.

WOULD YOU RATHER...

BE A BOY AND HAVE YOUR ENTIRE ROOM BE PINK

OR

BE A BOY AND WEAR ONLY PINK CLOTHES?

Until the mid-1900s, pink was considered a color for boys, and blue was for girls.

WOULD YOU RATHER...

HAVE EYEBROWS THAT MAKE A COMPLETE CIRCLE AROUND YOUR HEAD

OR

HAVE FLAT EYELASHES THAT STICK OUT 10 INCHES AND CANNOT BE TRIMMED?

Eyebrow hairs usually last between three and five months before you shed them.

In most cultures, long eyelashes are a sign of femininity.

WOULD YOU RATHER...

LiVE WiTH PARENTS WHO ARE CLEAN FREAKS

OR

WiTH PARENTS WHO ARE COMPLETE SLOBS?

- In the United States about 54 percent of people say they clean their house daily or weekly.

- And 98 percent say they feel good about themselves when their home is clean.

WOULD YOU RATHER

HAVE A CHICKEN THAT LAID GOLDEN EGGS EVERY WEEK

FIND A GIANT DIAMOND?

Q: How do chickens grow?

A: On eggplants.

The largest diamond
ever found was a
whopping 3,106 carats.
That's almost 1.5 pounds
of diamond.

WOULD YOU RATHER...

RUN YOUR TONGUE DOWN 10 FEET OF A NEW YORK CITY STREET

CLEAN YOUR BATHROOM WITH YOUR TONGUE?

When you flush the toilet, invisible germs are sprayed out of the bowl that can travel as much as 6 feet through the air. This means germs can land on toothbrushes, towels, doorknobs, and just about anything else in the bathroom.

RUN IN AN OLYMPIC MARATHON

OR

RIDE YOUR BICYCLE IN THE TOUR DE FRANCE?

The first Olympics were held in 776 B.C. and had only one event: a foot race where people ran naked.

Each year more than 100 professional cyclists ride in the Tour de France, which is over 2,000 miles long and takes 21 days to ride!

WOULD YOU RATHER...

CUT YOUR OWN HAIR

OR

GET IT CUT BY AN EXPERT HAIRDRESSER WHO IS BLINDFOLDED?

Before modern medicine came along, men who cut hair were also the ones to perform surgery, do bloodletting, and take care of people's teeth (usually by pulling them!).

WOULD YOU RATHER...

Ride a bull in the *OR* **Be the rodeo clown who tries to get the bull's attention?**

The most common injury for a bull rider is a concussion. And because most riders refuse to wear helmets, it's even more likely they'll hurt their head.

One type of rodeo clown is the barrel man. He has a big padded barrel that he can easily jump in and out of to protect himself when an angry bull charges.

Be named after a cartoon character

OR

Have a popular cartoon character based on you?

Goofy was originally named Dippy Dawg, which was then changed to Dippy the Goof, and then, eventually, just Goofy.

WOULD YOU RATHER...

HAVE TO SEW ALL YOUR OWN CLOTHES

HAVE TO GROW AND HUNT ALL YOUR OWN FOOD?

The modern sewing machine was invented in the 1850s. Before then, all sewing was done by hand.

In one year the average person in the United States will eat 187 pounds of fresh vegetables, 132 pounds of fresh fruits, 116 pounds of red meat, 65 pounds of poultry, and 244 eggs.

ALWAYS HAVE TO PICK YOUR NOSE WHEN RIDING IN A CAR

OR

ALWAYS HAVE TO SPIT ON PEOPLE WHEN YOU SPEAK TO THEM?

• About 17 percent of Americans say they've picked their nose while driving. Twice as many men as women pick their nose while driving.

• A healthy body makes a constant supply of spit. The average person produces enough saliva each day to fill a 12-ounce soda can.

Have to change your little brother's diapers **OR** Clean your grandmother's false teeth?

The average baby will have his diaper changed 7,300 times by age 2!

Cleaning false teeth (or dentures, as they're often called) is pretty much like cleaning real teeth—except they need to be soaked as well as brushed.

GET A PAPER CUT ON YOUR TONGUE

OR

HAVE A BOOGER IN YOUR NOSE ALL DAY THAT YOU CAN'T QUITE REACH?

One urban legend tells the story of a woman who cut her tongue while licking an envelope. Later, her tongue swelled up, and a live cockroach crawled out. Turns out there were cockroach eggs on the envelope glue that got into her tongue! Luckily, this story is 100 percent false.

WOULD YOU RATHER...

BE A VAMPIRE

OR

A WEREWOLF?

Q: What do you get if you cross a snowman and a vampire?

A: Frostbite.

WOULD YOU RATHER...

HAVE SUPERPOWERFUL EYES

OR

SUPERPOWERFUL EARS?

An owl has really powerful eyesight.
Even when it's almost completely dark out,
an owl can spot a mouse moving
from more than 150 feet away.

WOULD YOU RATHER...

BE AT A BASEBALL GAME AND TRY TO CATCH A FOUL BALL WITH A SOUP CAN

WITH YOUR SHIRT SLEEVE?

The best places to sit for catching foul balls are near the field, down by either the first or third base lines. You might be lucky enough to catch a grounder or a fly ball that's hit into the stands!

Have to wear a cape to school **OR** every day for a whole year

Have to wear pajamas with feet sewn on every time you go out to play for a whole year?

Although capes have been in and out of fashion over the centuries, they're best known for being worn by superheroes and vampires.

Did you know there are pajamas with feet made for adults?

Be 5 miles from shore on a deep lake stuck in a rowboat that has a slight but steady leak

OR

Be 1 mile high flying in a hot air balloon that has a slight but steady leak?

In 1988 Per Lindstrand set the record for highest flight in a hot air balloon. He got up to 65,000 feet, which is more than 12 miles up in the air!

217

SHARE YOUR HOME WITH A KOALA BEAR

OR

WITH A KANGAROO?

- A koala bear normally sleeps about 22 hours a day.

- A kangaroo can travel up to 30 feet in a single bound.

Never be able to chew gum again

OR

Always have to have gum in your mouth while you eat?

Did you know that rubber, the same substance that is in tires and pencil erasers, is an ingredient in some chewing gum?

In 1899 Franklin Canning invented the first chewing gum and called it Dentyne.

WOULD YOU RATHER...

OWN A PRIVATE JET WITH A PILOT READY TO FLY YOU AROUND WHENEVER YOU LIKE

OR

HAVE PARENTS WHO OWN A MAJOR LEAGUE BASEBALL TEAM?

The Washington Nationals, one of the major league baseball teams, was sold in May 2006 to a group of people for 450 million dollars.

TAKE A LONG, BUMPY RIDE IN A SMALL SHOPPING CART

OR

A SHORT RIDE IN A CEMENT TRUCK, IN THE PART THAT USUALLY HOLDS THE CEMENT ... WHICH IS EMPTY NOW BUT TURNING?

Each year in the United States
about 17,300 kids under age five
go to the emergency room to be treated
for injuries from shopping carts—
falls from shopping carts
are actually one of the
leading causes of
injury to small kids.

Wake up to find that your neck has grown 5 inches longer

OR

That your rear end has doubled in size?

If we continued to grow at the same rate that we do when we're very young, the average person would be about 20 feet tall!

WOULD YOU RATHER...

Never be able to eat a KitKat **OR** Never be able to eat M&M's again?

Around the world, 418 KitKat bars are eaten every second.

An estimated 400,000,000 M&M's are sold each day in the United States.

WOULD YOU RATHER...

LIVE AT THE TOP OF MOUNT RUSHMORE

OR

AT THE BOTTOM OF THE GRAND CANYON?

- On Mount Rushmore the presidents' mouths are 18 feet wide!

- The Grand Canyon is 6,000 feet deep at its deepest point, 15 miles across at its widest point, and 277 miles long.

Put on a pair of shoes filled with duck droppings

OR

Put on a hat full of raw eggs?

Duck poop makes an excellent fertilizer.

Raw eggs are actually very good for your hair and can be used as a conditioner.

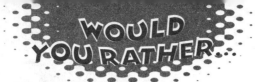
WOULD YOU RATHER...

ALWAYS HAVE A LOUD, DRIPPING FAUCET IN YOUR HOUSE

OR

HAVE A BUNCH OF ROOSTERS THAT LIVE NEARBY AND CROW LOUDLY EVERY MORNING?

Even a small leak in a faucet can waste up to 50 gallons of water a day. That's enough water to run a dishwasher twice.

Roosters are most famous for crowing at the break of day, but they also crow during the rest of the day and sometimes even at night.

WOULD YOU RATHER...

BE A STUNT PERSON
AND HAVE TO
JUMP OFF A CLIFF
WITH A PARACHUTE

HAVE TO JUMP OFF
WITHOUT A PARACHUTE
ONTO A GIANT
AIR-FILLED CUSHION?

Approximately one in 1,000 parachutes
doesn't open properly. That's why
you should always strap on
a backup parachute!

WOULD YOU RATHER...

Have a corn kernel stuck in between **OR** A celery string stuck around one tooth?

every tooth

An ear of corn is 80 percent water.

There is actually a celery-flavored soda called Cel-Ray.

WOULD YOU RATHER...

HAVE AN UGLY WART ON YOUR BiG TOE FOR TWO WEEKS

OR

A BiG PiMPLE ON THE TiP OF YOUR NOSE FOR THREE DAYS?

- Covering a wart with a piece of duct tape for a week is a surprisingly good way to get rid of it—it works 85 percent of the time.

- Many people swear that putting toothpaste on pimples makes them go away faster.

LiVE IN A HOUSE MADE OUT OF CHOCOLATE

OR

IN A HOUSE MADE OUT OF LiCORiCE?

A "chocolate house" was built in London, England in 1657— but it was a chocolate-maker's shop, *not* a house made of chocolate!

In the United States, the most common type of licorice candy is black licorice.

WOULD YOU RATHER...

Sit in a pit full of worms OR **Live in a room filled with rats for a week?** for a day

Worms don't have eyes, but they can sense light. They don't like light, however, because if they're in it for more than about an hour, they become paralyzed.

Rats can go without water longer than a camel can.

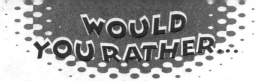
HAVE YOUR SCHOOL PICTURE TAKEN JUST AS YOU ARE MAKING A REALLY STUPID FACE

BE SICK THAT DAY AND NOT GET IN THE CLASS PICTURE THAT YEAR AT ALL?

You know that really funny face people make where they stick out their lower jaw as far as they can, cover their upper lip with their lower lip, and make their eyes look all crazy? It's called a gurn, and there are actually contests held to find the best gurn.

WOULD YOU RATHER...

BE THE SIZE OF A QUARTER AND HAVE TO RUN ACROSS THE PLAYING AREA OF A PINBALL MACHINE DURING A GAME

ACROSS AN AIR HOCKEY TABLE DURING A GAME?

Pinball machines are usually about 5 feet long and 2.5 feet wide, and there's a lot going on inside a pinball machine.

Air hockey tables are usually 8 feet long and 4 feet wide.

HAVE BODY ODOR SO BAD THAT iT CAN BE SMELLED FROM ACROSS THE YARD BUT NOT BE ALLOWED TO WEAR DEODORANT

OR

BE AS HAiRY AS A GORiLLA?

- Wiping your armpits with vinegar is thought to be a natural way to get rid of BO, because it can kill the bacteria that cause the odor.

  - The only parts of a gorilla that aren't covered by thick, dark hair are the face, ears, hands, and feet.

Live near a busy airport and have to listen to the roar of the airplanes

OR

Live near a city dump and have to smell the stinky garbage?

The world's busiest airport is currently Hartsfield-Jackson International Airport in Atlanta, Georgia.

Fresh Kills Landfill was once the world's largest dump. It was on Staten Island (a borough of New York City) and spanned 2,200 acres. Imagine living next to that!

WOULD YOU RATHER...

WAKE UP TOMORROW WITH A JACK-O'-LANTERN FOR A HEAD

WITH TREE LIMBS FOR ARMS AND LEGS?

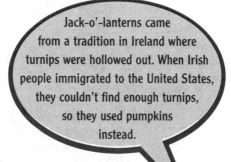

Jack-o'-lanterns came from a tradition in Ireland where turnips were hollowed out. When Irish people immigrated to the United States, they couldn't find enough turnips, so they used pumpkins instead.

SWIM IN FREEZING WATER

OR

IN A WARM SWIMMING POOL WHERE LOTS OF CHILDREN HAVE BEEN PEEING?

Fresh urine is cleaner than both spit and skin because healthy urine doesn't have bacteria in it.

NEVER BE ABLE TO EAT PIZZA AGAIN

OR

ALWAYS HAVE TO EAT ANCHOVIES ON ANY PIZZA YOU ATE?

In the United States pepperoni is the most popular pizza topping, and anchovies are the least favorite.
In Japan the preferred pizza topping is squid!

WOULD YOU RATHER...

**HAVE TO TRY
TO FIGHT OFF A MEAN DOG
USING ONLY A GIANT SQUIRT GUN ...
AND HAVE NO MORE WATER
FOR REFILLS**

**USING 20 CANS
OF SILLY STRING?**

Some of the bigger
water guns can hold
up to 100 ounces.
That's three-quarters
of a gallon of water!

Some cans of Silly String
supposedly produce
500 feet of string.

BE RUNNING AS FAST AS YOU CAN AND TRIP, LANDING FACE-FIRST IN A PATCH OF GRASS

OR

BE RUNNING ONLY HALF AS FAST AND TRIP, LANDING FACE-FIRST ONTO A BUNCH OF GRAVEL?

- If you slide on grass, your skin and clothes will probably get covered in green spots, called grass stains.

  - If you fall or slide on hard surfaces like gravel, you will get lots of tiny scrapes and cuts. This is often called road rash.

WOULD YOU RATHER...

TRY TO WIN A MILLION-DOLLAR PRIZE BY TWIRLING A HULA HOOP FOR FIVE MINUTES WITHOUT STOPPING

OR

BY JUMPING ON A POGO STICK ACROSS A FOOTBALL FIELD WITHOUT STOPPING OR FALLING?

The world record for hula-hooping is held by Roxann Rose, who hula-hooped in 1987 for an amazing 90 hours straight (that's almost four days!).

The regulation NFL football field is 360 feet long and 160 feet wide.

WOULD YOU RATHER...

Have to pick your nose every ten minutes for an entire day, no matter where you were

OR

Get a noogie from someone every five minutes for an entire day?

Compulsive nose-picking is called rhinotillexomania.

Noogies are sometimes called Dutch Rubs.

Never be able to eat your favorite food again

OR

Always have to stand on your head whenever you eat any food?

A typical stomach deals with about 50 tons of food during a lifetime.

Even if you eat while standing on your head, the food will still find its way to your stomach.

243

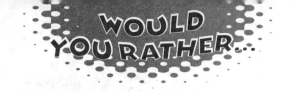

WOULD YOU RATHER...

Get tangled up in an OR octopus's arms

Have a baby elephant sit on you?

Octopuses are highly intelligent animals and are quite strong for their size.

It is common for a baby elephant to weigh 265 pounds at birth.

WOULD YOU RATHER...

ALWAYS HAVE A LITTLE GREEN PIECE OF SPINACH STUCK BETWEEN YOUR FRONT TEETH

ALWAYS HAVE A LITTLE BOOGER IN YOUR NOSE THAT MOVES WHEN YOU BREATHE?

Etiquette books say that if you get something stuck in your teeth while eating, you should politely excuse yourself and go to the bathroom to remove it. Whatever you do, don't just reach in with your finger and pick it out at the table—that's rude!

GET A PET PIG AS A PRESENT FROM YOUR PARENTS

OR

A BIG PET SNAKE?

Most snakes eat rodents, frogs, or insects. As a snake owner, you'd be responsible for finding these delightful things and feeding them to your adorable pet!

Pigs "root" in the trash and out in the yard, and pretty much anyplace else they think there's food. They can even learn to open cupboards and the fridge!

WOULD YOU RATHER...

GET PICKLE JUICE IN YOUR EYE

OR

LEMON JUICE IN YOUR PAPER CUT?

- Pickle juice has lots of salt, vinegar, and spices in it, and you can drink it to stop muscle cramps. But don't get it in your eye—that'll really sting and burn!

- During the Renaissance in Europe, some fashionable women put lemon juice on their mouth to make their lips redder.

WOULD YOU RATHER...

Not be able to read or Not be able to talk?

It is thought that more than 40 million adults in the United States cannot read.

A common speech problem is stuttering, which makes it hard to get words out. About 7 percent of people stutter at some time in their life.

WOULD YOU RATHER...

SUDDENLY TURN INTO A DOLPHIN AND BE IN THE OCEAN

SUDDENLY TURN INTO A MONKEY AND BE IN THE RAIN FOREST?

Most scientists agree that dolphins are very intelligent. They are thought to be smarter than dogs, and perhaps as smart as some monkeys and apes.

One of the ways that monkeys express affection is to groom each other. Of course, grooming also helps keep their fur clean of dirt and parasites.

249

Have four noses on your face **OR** Have a tongue as long as your body?

A slug has four noses.

A chameleon's tongue can be up to twice as long as its body.

Try to trim the beard **OR** Try to polish the tusks of a wild billy goat of a walrus?

Many male goats give off a very strong smell, which smells really good to female goats but smells terrible to people.

Walruses use their long tusks for fighting and to pull themselves out of the water.

WOULD YOU RATHER...

GET TRAPPED IN A CAVE FULL OF BATS

OR

SWIM IN A LAKE FULL OF LEECHES?

- **Bats can detect food from 18 feet away.**

- **A leech can drink up to five times its body weight in blood.**

Place first in the Olympics but have the gold medal **OR** taken away from you one year later

Win second place but get to keep your silver medal forever?

Q: What do you call the person who comes in second in a race to the top of a hill?

A: A runner-up.

WOULD YOU RATHER...

TURN INTO A FLY

OR

TURN INTO A COCKROACH?

A housefly can fly about 4.5 miles per hour, but they usually live for only two weeks.

Roaches spend 75 percent of their time just resting.

HAVE TO WEAR DiAPERS FOR THE REST OF YOUR LiFE

ALWAYS HAVE TO DRiNK AND EAT OUT OF A BABY BOTTLE?

The average baby needs its diaper changed eight to 12 times a day.

WOULD YOU RATHER...

Walk in circles through a revolving door 1,000 times

OR

Chew the same piece of gum for an entire week?

The first revolving door was invented in 1888 by Theophilus Van Kannel of Philadelphia, Pennsylvania.

The average person in the United States chews 190 sticks of gum every year.

WOULD YOU RATHER...

LIVE NEXT DOOR TO A HAUNTED HOUSE

ACROSS THE STREET FROM A CEMETERY?

One of the most famous movies about a haunted house is *The Amityville Horror*. Many people think the movie is based on a true story, but it's not—it's pure fiction.

There's an old superstition that you should always hold your breath when you pass a cemetery—to prevent evil spirits from entering your body.

WOULD YOU RATHER...

ALWAYS TAKE BATHS IN A TUB FILLED WITH POISONOUS SNAKES

ALWAYS SHOWER WITH WATER THAT HAS A LITTLE BIT OF SNAKE VENOM IN IT?

The record for sitting in a bathtub with the most live rattlesnakes is held by Jackie Bibby, who sat in a tub filled with 81 of them in 2005.

258

GROW UP TO BE A SCATOLOGIST

OR

AN ENTOMOLOGIST?

- A scatologist is someone who studies poop.

- An entomologist is someone who studies bugs.

ALWAYS HAVE A CAT SITTING ON YOUR HEAD

OR

ALWAYS WEAR AN ORANGE TRAFFIC CONE ON YOUR HEAD AND BIKE REFLECTORS ALL OVER YOUR CLOTHES?

Cats have a strong sense of balance and, if they do fall, they almost always can land on their feet.

Traffic cones were invented in 1914 by Charles P. Rudabaker, and were first made out of concrete. Try wearing that cone on your head!

WOULD YOU RATHER...

HAVE 14 FINGERS

OR

16 TOES?

Fingernails grow more quickly than toenails do.

Having extra fingers or toes is called polydactyly.

WOULD YOU RATHER...

LIVE AT THE BASE OF A VOLCANO

LIVE IN A PLACE WHERE THERE ARE LOTS OF TORNADOES?

When a powerful volcano erupts, it can shoot ash as high as 31 miles in the air.

In 1925 the worst tornado tragedy ever occurred in the Midwestern states of Missouri, Illinois, and Indiana. Several tornadoes formed and killed 747 people.

WOULD YOU RATHER...

Always feel like you almost have to sneeze

or

Have everything that touches you tickle?

Between 25 and 30 percent of people sneeze when they're exposed to light.

You can't tickle yourself, but nobody has ever been able to figure out why.

WOULD YOU RATHER...

HAVE CLUMPS OF HAIR GROWING ON YOUR TONGUE

HAVE REALLY LONG HAIR GROWING ON THE OUTSIDE OF YOUR NOSE?

Your tongue actually does have very tiny hairs on it that help you taste things.

As men get older, sometimes the hair in their nose starts to grow longer.

JUMP INTO A BATHTUB FULL OF ICE WATER

OR

FULL OF REALLY WARM SPIT?

The temperature of ice water is about zero degrees Celsius.

The average person will make enough spit in a lifetime to fill more than one swimming pool.

Never be allowed to **OR** Drink as much soda as you want, but sometimes find a fly in it?

7-Up was originally called
Bib-Label Lithiated
Lemon-Lime Soda.

Coca-Cola can be used
to clean a toilet bowl,
remove rust from metal, and
remove grease from clothes.

WOULD YOU RATHER...

LIVE IN A WORLD WITH NO CHAIRS

OR

WITH NO TABLES?

- Chairs were once used only by the very rich and powerful. Before the 16th century it wasn't common for everyone to have chairs in their homes.

- Without chairs, many tables wouldn't be very useful.

Tap dance for 24 hours without stopping

OR

Walk backward for an entire week?

Many people walk backward for exercise because it improves balance and works different muscles than the ones you use when you walk forward.

WOULD YOU RATHER...

BE FORBIDDEN TO EAT ANY CANDY, COOKIES, OR ICE CREAM FOR A WHOLE YEAR, BUT BE ALLOWED TO EAT ANYTHING ELSE YOU WANT

BE ALLOWED TO EAT ALL THOSE TREATS, BUT ALSO HAVE TO EAT THREE SERVINGS A DAY OF BROCCOLI OR CAULIFLOWER?

Broccoli and cauliflower look like miniature trees and are some of the coolest-looking veggies around. Have you ever seen yellow cauliflower or purple broccoli? They're even more fun to eat!

BE VERY CLUMSY

OR

BE VERY FORGETFUL?

- Everyone is clumsy—a normal person usually does something clumsy once or twice a day.

  - There's a condition called amnesia that makes it hard to remember new things, but some rare types of amnesia make you forget *everything* about your past.

WOULD YOU RATHER...

Sleep each night with two harmless bats in your bedroom

OR

Always have five pigeons hanging out in your bathroom?

Bats are very clean animals. They groom themselves regularly— just like cats do.

Pigeons are thought to be one of the smartest birds around, and they have been used for centuries to carry letters to faraway places.

Never again be able to celebrate the winter holidays

OR

Never again be able to celebrate your birthday?

Think of all the holidays that happen during the winter: Chanukah, Christmas, Kwanzaa, Ramadan, New Year's, Groundhog Day, Chinese New Year, Valentine's Day, Presidents Day, and maybe your birthday too!

WOULD YOU RATHER...

RIDE IN A TIGHTLY CLOSED, SMALL BOX ON A PLANE FOR 24 HOURS STRAIGHT

RIDE WITH PIGS IN THE BACK OF A TRUCK ON A TWO-DAY TRIP?

The fear of being trapped in a small or enclosed space is called claustrophobia.

Pigs are very clean animals, despite their messy reputation. And they don't like to go to the bathroom anywhere near where they live or eat.

273

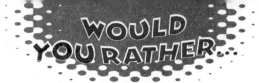

WOULD YOU RATHER...

Walk barefoot over a giant pile of dog poop  Over a bunch of live roaches?

The world's largest known roach was found in South America. It was six inches long and had a 1-foot wingspan!

WOULD YOU RATHER...

LIVE ON THE PLANET NEPTUNE

OR

ON VENUS?

Neptune is the windiest planet, with winds that blow as fast as 1,200 miles per hour.

Venus is the hottest planet in our solar system, with temperatures more than 800 degrees Fahrenheit.

WOULD YOU RATHER...

Run a mile over a OR **Swim across a lake of maple syrup that is 12 feet deep?** **6-inch layer of potatoes**

About 80 percent of a potato is water.

Maple syrup is about 67 percent sugar.

Never be able to smile

OR

Never be able to have dreams when you sleep?

You use more muscles to frown than you do to smile.

The average dream lasts only for two to three seconds!

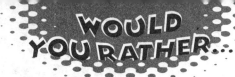

WOULD YOU RATHER...

**ALWAYS KEEP
ONE EYE CLOSED**

**BREATHE ONLY OUT
OF YOUR NOSE?**

Most people have just
one nostril working at a time
and, about every four hours,
one nostril takes over for
the other.

When a person has
only one eye it's called
being monocular.

NOT BE ABLE TO EAT THANKSGIVING DINNER EVER AGAIN

OR

FOR FIVE YEARS GET NO CARDS OR CANDY ON VALENTINE'S DAY?

No one is sure that turkey was actually part of the first Thanksgiving feast, but venison (that's deer meat) definitely was served.

About one billion Valentine's Day cards are sent each year.

LIVE IN AN ANT COLONY

OR

IN A BEEHIVE?

An ant colony can have as many as 500,000 ants in it.

A beehive can house up to 40,000 bees, but usually there aren't that many.

WOULD YOU RATHER...

That your ears were where your eyebrows are

OR

That your nose was where your belly button is?

Eyebrows are important. They keep things like dandruff and sweat from getting into your eyes.

HAVE TO SPEND SIX HOURS LYING IN A GUTTER ON THE SIDE OF A FLOODED STREET, WITH THE WATER SPLASHING OVER YOU

HAVE TO SPEND THE WHOLE DAY SITTING AT THE BOTTOM OF A PUBLIC TRASH CAN ON A CITY STREET, WITH PEOPLE DROPPING GARBAGE ON YOU EVERY FEW MINUTES?

More than 236 million tons of solid waste was produced in the United States in 2003. That means each person created an average of 4.5 pounds of garbage every day.

WOULD YOU RATHER...

Be a big slow bird *or* Be a fast little fish?

The slowest-flying birds are the American and the Eurasian woodcocks. They can fly at 5 miles per hour without stalling.

The fastest species of fish is believed to be the Indo-Pacific Sailfish, which can swim up to 68 miles an hour.

Lick the head of a sweaty, bald football player after a game

OR

Lick the whole top of a car hood that hasn't been washed in a month?

There's a Japanese sports drink called Pocari Sweat, but luckily it doesn't taste anything like sweat!

WOULD YOU RATHER...

HAVE TO WALK ON 5-FOOT STILTS FOR THE REST OF YOUR LiFE

OR

ALWAYS HAVE TO RiDE A UNICYCLE TO GET AROUND?

- In 2002 Doug Hunt set the world record for tallest stilts. He walked 29 steps on stilts that measured 50 feet 9 inches and weighed a total of 137 pounds.

- In 1968 Steve McPeak rode a unicycle all the way from Chicago to Los Angeles. The unicycle he rode was 32 feet high and the trip took six weeks.

WOULD YOU RATHER...

BE GREAT AT ONE SPORT BUT AWFUL AT ALL OTHERS

JUST BE OKAY AT ALL OF THEM?

A study showed that 53 percent of adults in the United States defined themselves as athletes.

Q: Why didn't the dog like to play football?

A: Because it was a boxer.

WOULD YOU RATHER...

Sleep on the sidewalk for seven nights straight during normal weather

OR

For one night when it's raining?

Normally, worms can't survive in the dry air above ground (they dry out very easily). But when it rains, it gets wet enough for them, and they come out to explore. That's why you see worms all over the sidewalk after a storm.

EAT A RAW STEAK THAT HAS BEEN LEFT ON A **OR** BUSY ROAD FOR AN HOUR

DRINK A GLASS OF JUICE THAT HAS BEEN SLOWLY POURED THROUGH THE WIG OF A SWEATY WOMAN WITH DANDRUFF?

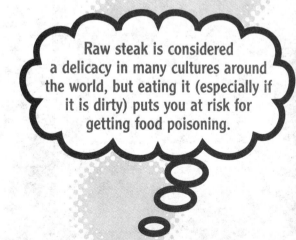

Raw steak is considered a delicacy in many cultures around the world, but eating it (especially if it is dirty) puts you at risk for getting food poisoning.

Be friends with a witch

OR

Be friends with a giant?

Throughout the ages, witches have supposedly been able to do all kinds of crazy things like casting spells, talking to plants, moving things with their minds, talking to the dead, healing sick people, and predicting the future.

In stories giants are often portrayed as stupid and violent, but there are real people who have a condition that makes them grow to be giant sized. Other than their size, these people are just like everyone else.

WOULD YOU RATHER...

HAVE TO TRY TO SMASH THREE ATTACKING RATTLESNAKES WITH ONLY A BOWLING BALL

TRY TO SIT STILL WHILE THOUSANDS OF HONEYBEES LAND ON YOUR FACE, FORMING A BEARD?

Rattlesnakes can feel vibrations in the ground, so they know when someone is coming.

More people die each year from bee stings than from snake attacks.

WOULD YOU RATHER...

BE STRANDED AT SEA
ON A GOOD, SAFE BOAT
WITH NO FOOD

OR

BE STRANDED AT SEA
ON AN OLD, WORN-OUT RAFT,
BUT HAVE A BOX OF FOOD?

A typical human can live
without food for about a month.
The body uses fat and protein it has stored
to keep going, so the length of time you can
last depends on how fat you are!

WOULD YOU RATHER...

BE ALLOWED TO EAT ONLY ASPARAGUS-FLAVORED iCE CREAM

ONLY BROCCOLi CAKE?

Baskin Robbins once made a ketchup-flavored ice cream.

Broccoli is a vegetable that's also a flower.

GET UP ONE MORNING AND
OPEN YOUR DRESSER DRAWERS,
AND SEE 100 BLACK WIDOW SPIDERS
RUN OUT

SEE 10 LARGE RATS RUN OUT AND
HIDE UNDER THE FURNITURE, BEHIND
THE DRAPES, AND IN THE CLOSET?

The black
widow spider's venom
is far more toxic than the
venom of a prairie rattlesnake, but
the black widow's bite is usually not
deadly because only a tiny amount
of venom is injected.

LIVE FOR THE REST OF YOUR LIFE ON THE MOON

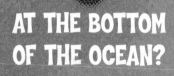

OR

AT THE BOTTOM OF THE OCEAN?

There's very little gravity on the moon, so you (and everything else) would be floating all the time. That might be fun, but it would also totally change the way you live. You'd have to come up with different ways to do almost everything—from eating to moving.

WOULD YOU RATHER...

LAUGH WHEN YOU SHOULD CRY AND CRY WHEN YOU SHOULD LAUGH

OR

NEVER BE ABLE TO DO EITHER ONE?

- On average, adults laugh 15 times a day, while kids usually laugh 400 times a day.

- The average person sheds 8 pints of tears in a year.

WOULD YOU RATHER...

Have to chop onions for a OR **Have to put onions on everything you ate for a whole month?**

week straight

Supposedly, if you chew gum while you're peeling onions, it'll keep you from crying.

Eating parsley will help you get rid of that stinky onion breath.

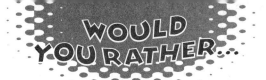

WOULD YOU RATHER...

HAVE TO WEAR GLASSES THAT MAKE ALL OF THE WORLD AROUND YOU LOOK VERY BEAUTIFUL BUT ALL THE PEOPLE LOOK REALLY UGLY

WEAR GLASSES THAT MAKE ALL THE PEOPLE BEAUTIFUL BUT EVERYTHING ELSE REALLY UGLY AND GROSS?

When people say that someone is "looking at the world through rose-colored glasses" they mean that the person is cheerful and optimistic, even if there's no reason to be.

ALWAYS HAVE A LITTLE SOMETHING STUCK IN BETWEEN YOUR TEETH

ALWAYS HAVE A LITTLE DIRT IN YOUR EYE?

Flossing removes all kinds of things that lurk between your teeth—like bacteria and bits of food. Next to brushing, flossing every day is the best way to keep your teeth and gums healthy.

Having dirt in your eye can cause the surface of your eye to get little scratches on it, which is called corneal abrasion, and can cause blurred vision and soreness in your eye.

WOULD YOU RATHER...

Live in a world where nobody cleans up after their dog **OR** Where everybody, including you, has to do it bare-handed?

Some people think bioluminescent additives (chemicals that make things glow) should be put in dog's food, so that their poop will glow. That way, people could more easily avoid stepping in it!

WOULD YOU RATHER...

Eat only pizza at **OR** every meal

Have someone else always choose what you're going to eat?

The average kid in the United States eats about 46 slices of pizza a year.

In the United States people eat more pizza during the week of the Super Bowl than they do during any other week of the year.

WOULD YOU RATHER...

Pick a carpet clean with tweezers *or* **Trim the lawn with nail clippers** instead of vacuuming it / instead of mowing it?

In 1947 the world's oldest carpet was dug out of a burial mound in Siberia. The carpet is thought to be 2,500 years old!

When you mow the lawn, always be extra careful and wear plenty of safety gear. Every year nearly 80,000 people in the United States get hurt by lawn mowers and have to go to the hospital.

BE A BOY NAMED MUFFIN E. SIMS

OR

A GIRL NAMED CASPAR P. JASPER?

- The name Muffin comes either from the German word *muffe*, which is a kind of cake, or from the French word *mouflet*, meaning a soft bread.

- The name Jasper comes from Greek or Persian and means treasure holder.

WOULD YOU RATHER...

SPEND THE REST OF YOUR LIFE IN A SUBMARINE

OR

THE REST OF YOUR LIFE IN A SPACESHIP?

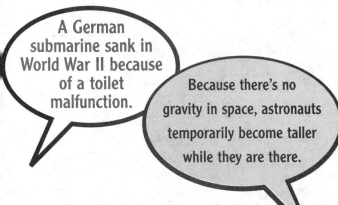

A German submarine sank in World War II because of a toilet malfunction.

Because there's no gravity in space, astronauts temporarily become taller while they are there.

HAVE TO SWALLOW A TINY WORM WITH EVERY MEAL YOU EAT

OR

LET 10 FLIES WALK OVER EVERY MEAL FOR AN HOUR BEFORE YOU EAT IT?

Worms can eat their own weight in food each day.

When flies are first hatched, they're called maggots. For many centuries maggots have been used to clean out wounds and heal sick people because they eat dead tissue and kill bacteria.

WOULD YOU RATHER...

Memorize a restaurant's menu, word for word

OR

Repeat out loud the same one word, of your choice, 5,000 times?

Restaurant menus as we know them didn't exist until the 19th century. Before then, menu choices were written on signs or chalkboards; and even before *then*, menu selections were unknown even to the waiters—everybody just ate whatever the chef gave them!

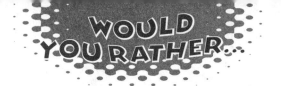

WOULD YOU RATHER...

BE REALLY ITCHY FOR A WHOLE DAY
AFTER LYING ON THE GRASS IN
SHORTS AND A T-SHIRT

HAVE SOMEONE CONSTANTLY GIVING
YOU A WET WILLY FOR
A WHOLE DAY?

Touching grass causes an allergic reaction in some people that makes their body itch.

A wet willy is when somebody puts their finger in their mouth to get it nice and slimy, and then sticks the icky finger in your ear!

THAT iT RAiNED CATERPiLLARS FOR ONE DAY

OR

THAT iT RAiNED FEATHERS EVERY DAY FOR A MONTH?

- Caterpillars grow faster than any other animal in the world. For example, a tobacco hornworm caterpillar's weight will increase 10,000 times in about 20 days.

- The Whistling Swan has the most feathers of any bird. In the winter, it can have as many as 25,000 feathers.

Eat a handful of human boogers

OR

Drink a cup of monkey spit?

In Great Britain, a booger is called a bogey.

There are many diseases, some very dangerous, that humans can catch from coming into contact with monkey spit.

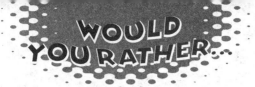

WOULD YOU RATHER...

WALK 10 MILES IN A SQUISHY SWAMP UP TO YOUR KNEES

WALK 10 MILES IN SNOW UP TO YOUR WAIST?

Ever wonder why swamps bubble? That's gas coming up from the bottom, which is produced when dead animals and plants break down in the muck.

The world's largest snow castle is built every winter in Kemi, Finland. It is so big that it has a theme park, a hotel, and even a chapel where you can get married.

WOULD YOU RATHER...

Have X-ray vision OR Be able to fly?

Comic-book superhero Superman can fly *and* has X-ray vision. He once used his special vision to see the color of Lois Lane's underwear!

WOULD YOU RATHER...

Lick all the computer keyboards at a public library

or

Lick the bench at a downtown bus stop?

The New York Public Library has more than 42,762,893 items and 1,788,286 users. Think twice about licking those keyboards!

WOULD YOU RATHER...

EAT FOUR SLICES OF MOLDY BREAD

OR

EAT ONE PIECE OF ROTTEN FRUIT?

- Some types of mold are edible, and mold is even used to make certain cheeses. Mold is what makes blue cheese blue.

- Sometimes overripe fruit is better for baking. When your bananas turn brown, stick them in the freezer and use them later to make banana bread.

Wake up one morning and discover that your body is **OR** covered with hundreds of snails

Wake up to find that your nose and ears are filled with a weird-smelling yellow slime?

The smallest-known snail is the Ammonicera rota, which measures about .02 of an inch.

The largest-known snail is the Giant African Land Snail. It can weigh up to two pounds and grow to be more than 15 inches long.

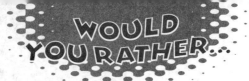
WOULD YOU RATHER...

HAVE A JAR OF JELLYBEANS THAT IS ALWAYS FULL

HAVE AN ENDLESS SUPPLY OF CHEWING GUM THAT NEVER LOSES ITS FLAVOR?

Jellybeans were invented at the beginning of the 20th century, but it wasn't until 1930 that the jellybean became associated with Easter, probably because of its egg shape.

Studies have shown that chewing gum helps people relax.

WOULD YOU RATHER...

LIVE IN A PLACE WHERE IT IS SUNNY 24 HOURS A DAY

OR

WHERE IT IS COMPLETELY DARK ALL DAY AND ALL NIGHT?

If the sun stopped shining, it would take eight minutes for people on Earth to notice a difference.

In parts of Alaska, during the winter it is dark 24 hours a day and during the summer there is sunlight around the clock.

315

WOULD YOU RATHER...

Eat three raw clams covered in grape jelly

OR

A cup of strawberry yogurt and tuna fish mixed together?

There are more than 2,000 varieties of clams. The tiniest clams are about the size of a fingernail and giant clams can be almost 4 feet long.

Tuna may not go well with strawberry yogurt, but it is the biggest-selling seafood in the United States.

WOULD YOU RATHER...

HAVE A GARDEN FILLED WITH BEAUTIFUL FLOWERS THAT DON'T SMELL GOOD

HAVE A REFRIGERATOR FULL OF FOOD THAT LOOKS DISGUSTING BUT TASTES DELICIOUS?

There are some flowers that smell like rotten meat!

Many people believe we "eat with our eyes," which means that when food doesn't look good to us, most likely it won't taste good to us.

SEE EVERYTHING UPSIDE DOWN

OR

HEAR EVERYTHING BACKWARD?

The human eye actually sees things upside down, but a message is immediately sent to our brain, which then allows us to see images right-side up so everything looks correct.

318

WOULD YOU RATHER...

Walk around for a year with six large OR **Wear bells on your fingers for five years?**

In 1982 a California man tied 42 weather balloons to a lawn chair and rose 16,000 feet in the air!

The Liberty Bell originally weighed 2,080 pounds, but now it's down to only 2,055 pounds. The missing 25 pounds was probably chiseled away from the inside of the bell by people who wanted to take a piece of history with them.

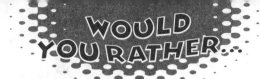

WOULD YOU RATHER...

Be forced to drink like a dog, licking up liquids with your tongue **OR** **Be forced to eat all your food without using a fork, spoon, or knife?**

Dogs' floppy tongues make it easy for them to lick and drink out of a bowl, but the human tongue is pretty short and clumsy, which makes it harder for us to slurp things up.

The spork, a combination of a spoon and fork, is pretty common, but have you ever heard of a knork? It's a knife combined with a fork.

WOULD YOU RATHER...

HAVE TO RUN 5 MILES AS FAST AS YOU CAN ON A TRAIL COVERED WITH A 1-INCH LAYER OF HONEY

OR

ON A TRAIL COVERED WITH POPCORN UP TO YOUR KNEES?

- Honey is the only food that doesn't spoil.

- When popcorn pops, it can fly as high as 3 feet into the air.

Be asked to star in a movie **or** Be asked to join your favorite band?

with your favorite actor

Q: Why are movie stars always so cool?

A: Because they have lots of fans!

WOULD YOU RATHER...

BE ATTACKED BY A BUNCH OF ANGRY LOBSTERS

BY A PACK OF ANGRY RACCOONS?

The average adult lobster is 9 inches long and weighs between 1.5 and 2 pounds.

The average adult raccoon weighs 21 pounds.

TAKE A BITE OUT OF A LIVE FROG

OR

SWALLOW A LIVE BABY SNAKE?

Wrestling a live frog into your mouth is tricky. Plus, many frogs produce chemicals that make them taste bad—not to mention making them possibly dangerous to bite. Cooked frogs' legs are eaten and considered a delicacy in many countries, including France.

BE A CHARACTER IN AN ADVENTURE MOVIE AND HAVE TO FIGHT A DRAGON

HAVE TO FIGHT A WIZARD?

In the book and film version of *Harry Potter and the Goblet of Fire,* the lovable kid wizard, Harry, must battle a vicious, fire-breathing dragon, the Hungarian Horntail, during the Triwizard Tournament.

Have the bad
habit of
licking your scratching
fingers too
much when
you eat

Have the bad
habit of
your behind
a lot?

Even before the invention of
knives and forks, licking your
fingers was considered rude.

Here's some advice:
If you scratch your behind,
don't bite your fingernails!

Sleep every night on a hammock that is **OR** hung three stories up in the air

Sleep every night on a pool mattress floating in a pond filled with little baby sharks?

During one of the Apollo lunar landing missions, the astronauts hung hammocks in the spacecraft so they could sleep between moonwalks.

Baby great white sharks are already about 5 feet long at birth; once they're full grown they're often three times that length.

WOULD YOU RATHER...

CHEW ON A MARBLE-SiZED HAIRBALL THAT YOUR CAT COUGHED UP

ON A MARBLE-SiZED WAD OF SOMEBODY'S EARWAX?

In 2004 an 18-year-old woman from Canada had surgery to remove a 5-pound hairball from her lower intestine.

Many whales have a buildup of earwax, often adding up to four layers of wax every year.

WOULD YOU RATHER...

EAT AT A RESTAURANT TABLE DIRECTLY UNDER AN ELECTRIC BUG ZAPPER

DIRECTLY UNDER THE EDGE OF THE ROOF WHERE ALL THE BIRDS STICK OUT THEIR BUTTS?

Some scientists say that bug zappers actually do more harm than good. The zappers kill only a few of the biting bugs, and they zap tons of harmless bugs that might otherwise eat those pesky mosquitoes.

Have no OR Have 12 kids?

Have you seen any movies lately about families with loads of kids— like *Cheaper by the Dozen* (12 kids), *Cheaper by the Dozen 2* (20 kids), or *Yours, Mine and Ours* (18 kids)?

Catch a porcupine thrown **OR** from a second-story window

Get sprayed by a skunk?

A porcupine can have as many as 30,000 quills—and they're all sharp!

A spotted skunk will often do a handstand before it sprays.

WOULD YOU RATHER...

HAVE TO EAT A RAW GOLDFISH AND CHEW IT UP COMPLETELY

LICK THE BOTTOMS OF A MAN'S DIRTY, SMELLY FEET?

If you keep a goldfish in a dark room, it will turn white.

The bottoms of your feet and the palms of your hands cannot grow hair.

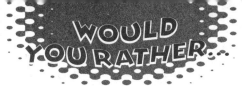

That your family be forced to drive an air-polluting car with a muffler that spews smoke That your family be forced to throw all their garbage into a local stream?

Cars are much more environmentally friendly than they used to be. These days, 20 new cars produce the same amount of pollution that only one car from the 1960s produced.

WOULD YOU RATHER...

Be hit in the face with a baseball-sized water balloon full of blue paint

OR

Wake up with a big wad of chewed bubble gum stuck in your hair?

On April 22, 2006, at the Xbox 360 Water Balloon Challenge on Sydney's Coogee Beach in Australia, more than 2,900 gamers threw about 55,000 balloons and set the record for the largest water balloon fight ever!

In Singapore, it is against the law to make or sell chewing gum.

WOULD YOU RATHER...

HAVE TO WALK A TIGHTROPE BETWEEN TWO REALLY TALL BUILDINGS

HAVE TO JUMP FROM ONE HIGH TRAPEZE TO ANOTHER TO GET ACROSS TWO REALLY TALL BUILDINGS . . . WITH NO NET?

French tightrope walker Charles Blondin first crossed Niagara Falls in 1859. He later walked across it blindfolded and then again pushing a wheelbarrow!

Jules Léotard invented the flying trapeze act in the late 19th century, and later the leotard was named after him.

That all your favorite foods **OR** Get sick whenever you are near any type of animal?

Even something as delicious as ice cream makes some people sick. That's usually because they are either allergic to milk or lactose intolerant.

There are a lot of people who *do* get sick when they're around certain animals. About 15 percent of people are allergic to cats or dogs.

WOULD YOU RATHER...

Never be allowed to wear socks

OR

Never be allowed to wear underwear?

Your feet have about 500,000 sweat glands, and sweat more than a pint a day.

In the 19th century, men often wore union suits, which was a kind of one-piece underwear that covered them from their necks to their ankles. Luckily, the suits had a flap that opened in the back that made going to the bathroom a bit easier.

BE THE WORLD'S TALLEST PERSON

OR

THE WORLD'S SHORTEST PERSON?

- The tallest person on record was Robert Pershing Wadlow. He was 8 feet 11 inches tall.

- The shortest person on record was Gul Mohammed of India. He was only 22.5 inches tall.

HAVE TO TAKE A BATH FOR A HALF HOUR WITH A SNAPPING TURTLE IN THE TUB

WITH ONE LITTLE BABY TIGER SHARK IN THE WATER WITH YOU?

The snapping turtle is America's largest freshwater turtle. Their shells can be up to 18 inches long.

Tiger sharks battle each other while still in their mother's womb, and the survivor is the newborn baby shark.

EAT A LARGE BUCKET OF LIVE SPIDERS

OR

A HUGE PLATTER OF RAW, MOLDY BACON?

- Almost all spiders produce venom that they use to kill their prey, but luckily most spiders aren't poisonous to humans.

  - In Ireland they eat something called back rashers, which is bacon made from the meat on the back of a pig.

WOULD YOU RATHER...

Run into a girl you have a crush on and be talking to her when you realize you're standing in a pile of dog poop

OR

Have her point out to you that you've got a bunch of ants and flies crawling all over you?

Ever wonder why dogs eat poop? If you can believe it, poop smells yummy to them! And poop, especially cat poop, is also very high in protein, so some dogs eat it if their regular diet doesn't give them enough protein.

A fear of insects is called entophobia.

Have a best friend who is always humming

OR

Who repeats everything you say right after you say it?

In Massachusetts it's illegal to feed ducks while humming on Sunday between the hours of 5 A.M. and 12 P.M. Do you wonder why that law was passed?

Some theater students practice a "repetition game" to help them improve their acting skills.

BE COVERED IN DOG FUR

OR

BE COVERED IN LIZARD SKIN?

Chameleons are known for their ability to change colors. Most people think chameleons change colors to blend in with their surroundings, but in fact their skin changes in response to temperature, light, and their mood.

Lick the sole of a dirty old flip-flop

OR

Lick the bottoms of all four of a dog's paws?

Two brothers, George and Ira Flop, invented the flip-flop in 1956.

The only sweat glands that dogs have are in between the pads of their paws.

WOULD YOU RATHER...

BE ON TV

OR

BE IN A VIDEO GAME?

In 1928 the United States became the first country to broadcast television.

In 1967 Ralph Baer invented the first video game, called Chase, that could be played on a TV.

WOULD YOU RATHER...

Live in a place where it is always raining **OR** In a place where it is always snowing?

The rainiest city in the United States is Hilo, Hawaii, with an average of 278 rainy days a year.

The snowiest U.S. city is Stampede Pass, Washington. It gets an average of 440.3 inches of snow a year!

HAVE TO TRY TO ESCAPE WHILE BEING CHASED BY WONDER WOMAN

WHILE BEING CHASED BY BATMAN?

Wonder Woman is 5 feet 11 inches tall, but she is not the tallest heroine in the DC Comics world. Superhero Big Barda is a whopping 7 feet tall.

Bruce Wayne (Batman) was named by *Forbes* as the seventh richest fictional character. The list also included other wealthy characters like Willy Wonka (*Willy Wonka & the Chocolate Factory*), Scrooge McDuck (whose nephew is Donald Duck), and Daddy Warbucks (*Annie*).

WOULD YOU RATHER...

EAT A HANDFUL OF GOOEY HAIRS PULLED FROM A CLOGGED SHOWER DRAIN

A COUPLE OF BUGS THAT WERE PICKED OFF A MONKEY'S BEHIND?

That pink area on a monkey's behind is called a rump pad.

Be a bug that just got caught in **OR** a spider's web

Be a fly in a small room being chased by a lady with a flyswatter?

Besides the traditional flyswatter, there is also a fly gun, which uses a spring-loaded disk to "swat" flies, and an electric flyswatter, which delivers electric shocks to flies!

WOULD YOU RATHER...

Know your own future

OR

Know the future of your friends and not be able to tell them?

Predictions about the future can cause you to change your behavior, and maybe even fulfill your fortune—a self-fulfilling prophecy!

WOULD YOU RATHER...

GOBBLE LiKE A TURKEY FOR THREE HOURS EVERY THANKSGIVING DAY WITHOUT BEING ABLE TO EXPLAIN WHY YOU ARE DOING iT

OR

BE DRESSED iN A TURKEY COSTUME FOR THE WHOLE DAY EVERY THANKSGIVING . . . BUT BE FREE TO SPEAK?

• Only male turkeys gobble. Females make a clicking noise.

• A turducken is a turkey stuffed with a duck, stuffed with a chicken. Sounds pretty complicated—try dressing up as that for Halloween!

Have to drink a gallon of OR water from your own toilet (after you flush it)

Have to sit on a toilet for a week straight?

About 75 percent of people in the United States are chronically dehydrated, which means they're not drinking enough water.

U.S. President Lyndon Johnson supposedly liked to meet with his staff while he was on the toilet.

WOULD YOU RATHER...

HAVE YOUR PARACHUTE NOT OPEN ALL THE WAY AND COME DOWN TWICE AS FAST AS NORMAL, AND LAND IN A HUGE PILE OF STRAW

LAND IN THE DEEP END OF SOMEBODY'S SWIMMING POOL?

A typical parachute descends at approximately 18 feet per second.

If you fall faster than about 80 miles an hour, the force on your body from hitting water is about the same as if you slammed into concrete.

WOULD YOU RATHER...

ALWAYS SOUND EXTREMELY MEAN

OR

ALWAYS LOOK LIKE YOU'VE JUST SMELLED SOMETHING BAD?

The average person farts
14 times a day and excretes
about half a liter of fart gas.
So maybe you really did
smell something bad!

WOULD YOU RATHER...

DRIVE ALL THE WAY ACROSS THE UNITED STATES

OR

SAIL ACROSS THE ATLANTIC OCEAN TO EUROPE?

The driving distance between the East and West coasts of the United States is about 3,000 miles, depending on the route you take.

By sea, the trip from New York City, New York, to London, England, is a little more than 3,000 miles.

WOULD YOU RATHER...

Live in a place where it is sunny all the time but really windy

OR

A place where it is cloudy all the time but there is no wind?

Mount Washington, New Hampshire, is the windiest place in the United States.

Cold Bay, Alaska, is the cloudiest place in the United States.

WOULD YOU RATHER...

Accidentally suck a large fly through your nose and swallow it

OR

Have a tiny fly go inside your ear and never be able to get it out?

In the 1800s, a beetle crawled into the ear of a British man named John Hanning Speke. He practically went nuts trying get the bug out of his ear, but nothing worked. Finally, he stuck a knife in his ear. It killed the pesky beetle, but it really hurt his ear, which got infected and a hole developed between his ear and nose. After that, his ear would whistle loudly whenever he blew his nose!

WOULD YOU RATHER...

Pick your nose in public and have to eat it

OR

Pick someone else's nose in public but not have to eat it?

Some people don't blow their nose with a tissue or handkerchief. They hold one nostril closed and blow the boogers out the other nostril. This gross move is called a *snot rocket* or a *crunch and blow*.

WOULD YOU RATHER...

HAVE TO LICK A DIRTY PIG UNTIL IT IS CLEAN

OR

EAT FIVE LIVE BEETLES?

- In Thailand they eat Frizzy Pork Hair sandwiches for breakfast. Sounds pretty gross, except the "hair" is really just dried pork meat that's broken into very thin strands.

- In a lifetime the average person will accidentally eat about a pound of insects.

WOULD YOU RATHER...

Clip a stranger's **or** Chew your own dirty, disgusting toenails toenails?

If you don't cut your nails regularly, they can grow into your skin. That's called an ingrown nail.

About 15 percent of people secretly chew their toenails.

GO TO THE BATHROOM AND HAVE TO USE A ROLL OF TOILET PAPER THAT IS SOAKING WET

A DRY NEWSPAPER TO WIPE?

The average person uses 57 sheets of toilet paper each day.

Before modern toilet paper was invented, people used all kinds of crazy things to wipe their behinds: their hands (*EWWW!*), leaves, rags, snow, fruit skins, seashells (*ouch!*), sponges on sticks, and newspapers. But don't try these at home—you'll clog the toilet!

WOULD YOU RATHER...

Make 51 sand castles in one day

OR

Make 101 snowmen in one day?

The world's tallest snowman was built in Maine in 1999. His name was Angus, and he stood more than 113 feet tall. His eyes were made of wreaths, six car tires were used for his mouth, and two 10-foot trees were used for his arms.

HAVE HUGE, PUFFY BLOWFISH CHEEKS

GiANT BAT EARS?

Dolphins sometimes treat blowfish like toys. They tease the blowfish with their teeth. That scares the fish and makes them inflate, which entertains the dolphins.

Because bats can't see well, they use their ears to survive. They make high-pitched sounds and then listen to the echoes. This helps bats figure out where they are and where to hunt.

Swallow a handful of live tadpoles OR Eat a whole dead frog?

In France tadpole soup is a very popular dish!

If you drop a frog into a pot of boiling water, it will hop right out. But if you put it in a pot of cold water and then slowly heat the water, the frog will stay put and be boiled to death.

WOULD YOU RATHER...

HAVE SKIN LIKE AN ARMADILLO'S

OR

HAVE NORMAL SKIN BUT A 6-FOOT-LONG TAIL?

- For a little while, when human babies are still in the womb, they have tails! As the baby develops, the tail is usually absorbed into the body. But every once in a while people are born with their tails.

- A 12-year-old boy in Asia had the longest human tail—9 inches long!

Ride an elevator 1,000 feet up into the air **OR** Down 1,000 feet below the surface of the Earth?

The Eiffel Tower in France, which is about 990 feet tall, has double-decker elevators. They travel up the curved legs of the tower, but they're designed so that the cars remain level all the way up.

HAVE TO CATCH EVERY FISH IN A LARGE POND

FIND A NEEDLE IN A ROOM FILLED WITH JELL-O?

Jell-O is the official favorite snack food of Utah. Mormons are so well known for being fond of Jell-O that the parts of the western United States where they live is nicknamed the Jell-O Belt.

WOULD YOU RATHER...

BE EATING IN A RESTAURANT AND HAVE A WAITER WITH VERY DIRTY FINGERNAILS SERVING YOUR MEAL

HEAR THE CHEF'S BAD COUGH DURING THE WHOLE TIME YOU ARE EATING?

Only about two-thirds of Americans wash their hands after going to the bathroom—you'd better hope your waiter is in that group!

The blast of air created by a cough can move as fast as 300 miles per hour and can be chock-full of germs.

WOULD YOU RATHER...

BE A CARTOON CHARACTER AND HAVE TO TAKE YOUR CHANCES FIGHTING BATMAN

OR

TAKE YOUR CHANCES FIGHTING SPIDER-MAN?

Alain Robert, a man who has climbed more than 70 tall buildings using only his hands and feet, sometimes wears a Spider-Man suit when climbing and has earned the nickname Spider-Man.

EAT A SPOONFUL OF SOMEONE ELSE'S NOSE HAIR

OR

A SPOONFUL OF SOMEONE ELSE'S BELLY BUTTON LINT?

Belly button lint is usually made up of fibers from your clothes, strands of hair, and dead skin cells.

Be missing one of your fingertips

OR

Have a bucket stuck on your foot for a year?

Babies' fingertips are among the few body parts that can regrow. Unfortunately, this ability disappears after about age six.

In many Arab countries and in Thailand, it's very offensive to show someone the bottom of your foot.

371

SLEEP AS MUCH AS A CAT DOES

OR

NEVER NEED ANY SLEEP?

- Cats sleep more than any other mammal. They get an average of 16 hours of sleep a day.

- Sharks need to keep moving to breathe, so they're always swimming. This means that they're never asleep in the way that a human is.

Become famous for something **OR** that wasn't really your doing

See someone else become famous because of something you did?

Most people think Thomas Edison invented the lightbulb, but in fact several other people had come up with a version of a bulb before he did.

WOULD YOU RATHER...

SHARE YOUR HOME WiTH SiX 90-YEAR-OLD MEN AND SiX 90-YEAR-OLD WOMEN

OR

SHARE YOUR HOME WiTH TWO OSTRiCHES?

The ostrich is the largest type of bird around. It's big enough that small people (like kids) can ride them, but watch out! Some ostriches have bad tempers.

Always have to talk holding your tongue with your hand OR **Always have to keep a hand over one eye whenever you look at anything?**

Stephen Taylor has the longest tongue on record, measured in May 2002. It's 3.7 inches from the tip of his tongue to the center of his top lip.

Even though newborn babies can see their hands, they don't realize that their hands are part of their bodies. It isn't until they're about six weeks old that they begin to figure it out.

SUCK ON A FISH EYE FOR TEN MINUTES

EAT A HANDFUL OF TINY LIVE FISH?

Fish don't have eyelids.

Fish are slimy because their skin produces mucus to coat itself. The mucus helps protect the fish from getting sick and helps them swim faster.

WOULD YOU RATHER...

Always have to walk around in a sleeping bag OR **Always have to sleep in a bathtub?**

One popular sleeping bag design is the mummy bag. The shape follows the outline of a body—narrower at the feet than at the shoulders—like an Egyptian mummy.

Ever heard of a walk-in bathtub? It's smaller and deeper than a regular tub, and it has a door that you walk through to get into the tub.

WOULD YOU RATHER...

HAVE REALLY BAD DANDRUFF

OR

REALLY BAD ACNE?

- Apple cider vinegar, salt, and lemon juice all supposedly cure dandruff when left on the scalp for a while and then rinsed off.

  - Acne is a very common skin condition that causes people to get lots of pimples.

WOULD YOU RATHER...

Burst a huge bubble all over your face and then have to pick the bubble gum all off, little by little

OR

pick dried super glue off your fingers after spilling a whole tube of it on your hands?

In 1906 Frank Fleer invented the first bubble gum. It was called Blibber-Blubber, but it was never sold because it was too sticky.

If your fingers get glued together with super glue, you can use nail polish remover to dissolve the glue and free your fingers.

WOULD YOU RATHER...

HAVE AN EXTRA MOUTH PLACED IN THE MIDDLE OF YOUR STOMACH

OR

HAVE SIX FINGERS ON EACH HAND?

Antonio Alfonseca, a pitcher for the Texas Rangers, has six fingers on each hand and six toes on each foot. He's nicknamed El Pulpo, which means The Octopus in Spanish.

Get into bed every night by jumping on a trampoline and bouncing onto your bed or **By sliding down a fireman's pole from the second story onto your bed?**

It's believed that the first trampoline was created by Eskimos. They used walrus skin and tossed each other into the air, sort of like what firemen do when they catch people jumping out of burning buildings.

WOULD YOU RATHER...

GET EVERYWHERE BY CRAWLING

OR

HAVE TO STAND ON YOUR HANDS WHENEVER YOU ARE STANDING STILL?

- Normally crawling is done on your hands and knees, but *plastun* crawling is when you crawl with your whole body flat on the ground.

- Some people can do handstand push-ups. That's when you raise and lower yourself while standing on your hands. You need pretty strong arms to do that!

WOULD YOU RATHER...

Have hair made of straw **OR** Have a pig nose?

Straw isn't just useful in farming; it can be used as an energy source, in construction, and, of course, to make hats!

In English, we say a pig goes *oink*, but the sound a pig makes is different in other languages, for example: *chrum* (Polish), *hunk* (Albanian), and *hulu* (Mandarin Chinese).

WOULD YOU RATHER...

DRINK FRESH MILK DIRECTLY FROM A COW'S UDDER

DRINK STORE-BOUGHT MILK TWO DAYS AFTER IT HAS TURNED SOUR?

A cow's udder can hold almost 11 gallons of milk.

When milk sours, it eventually becomes very thick like yogurt, and can then be used in cooking.

LIVE IN A WORLD WHERE EACH WORD YOU SAY WILL COST YOU A PENNY

OR

WHERE EACH TIME YOU USE THE BATHROOM IT WILL COST YOU 10 CENTS?

It costs about 1.23 cents to produce one penny, which means it costs more to make them than they're worth!

In many cities in Europe, there are public toilets that you have to pay to use.

WOULD YOU RATHER...

Spend two weeks with your head stuck in a metal bucket One week with your entire body stuck between the bars of an iron fence?

Here's a kind of bucket you don't want stuck on your head: a honey bucket. That's what's put under the seat in an outhouse (like an old-fashioned porta-potty) to catch people's waste.

WOULD YOU RATHER...

HAVE A BABY THAT CRIES TWICE AS LOUD AND TWICE AS OFTEN AS OTHER BABIES

OR

ONE WHOSE DIAPER NEEDS TO BE CHANGED TWICE AS OFTEN BUT IS VERY QUIET AND WELL BEHAVED?

- From birth, babies have a built-in instinct to cry. It's how they show that they're hungry or uncomfortable, like when they have a wet diaper.

- In Great Britain, a diaper is called a nappy.

WOULD YOU RATHER...

Eat 3 cups of bacon fat

OR

Drink 3 cups of a St. Bernard's drool?

It's the fat that gives bacon most of its well-loved flavor.

A full-grown St. Bernard dog can weigh up to 200 pounds, and they're known for being big droolers.

EAT SWEAT-FLAVORED iCE CREAM

EAT A POOP-FLAVORED CANDY BAR?

As you can tell if you've ever tasted sweat, it has a lot of salt in it.

Lots of animals eat poop: rabbits, rodents, gorillas, bugs, and, of course, dogs.

Have one long, thick, furry eyebrow across your entire forehead

OR

Eyebrows with really long hair that cannot be trimmed?

A person with only one long eyebrow is said to have a unibrow. Long ago, some people were suspicious of anyone who had a unibrow because it was associated with werewolves.

The world record for the longest eyebrow hair was set in 1994 by Frank Ames: it was 3.7 inches long!

WOULD YOU RATHER...

Never stop talking all day long *OR* **Be able to say only 10 words each day?**

When someone talks all the time and can't control it, it's called logorrhea.

Women say an average of 7,000 words per day, and men say just over 2,000 words a day!

EAT AN UNCOOKED BUT THAWED TV DINNER

OR

A CAN OF COLD BEEF CHILI?

The TV dinner was invented by Gerry Thomas in 1954. It first came in an aluminum tray that you heated in an oven.

During the French Revolution, the French needed a way to get food to their troops without it going bad, so someone developed a method of vacuum-sealing food in glass jars. That invention eventually led to canning, which became a common way of preserving food.

HAVE A SMALL BUTT ON YOUR CHIN

OR

TWO LITTLE FEET DANGLING FROM YOUR NOSE?

A cleft chin—
a chin with a dimple
in the center of it—
is sometimes called
a butt chin.

Have to sleep in a room with a rat in it for a whole week

OR

Carry five roaches in your pocket for one day?

Although rats prefer to eat nutritious things like vegetables, fruit, and meat, they'll eat just about anything—even shoes!

Cockroaches can run faster than 3 miles per hour. That's the same as if a human sprinter could run more than 200 miles per hour!

WOULD YOU RATHER...

BE STUCK 100 FEET UP IN A BIG TREE AND BE RIGHT NEXT TO A HIVE OF BEES

BE RIGHT ABOVE AN ANGRY NESTING EAGLE?

Bees perform complicated dances to talk with each other about things like where they can find good food.

Eagles have very large beaks that are hooked, which makes it easier for them to tear the flesh off their prey.

WOULD YOU RATHER...

EAT ONE LIVE TARANTULA

OR

HOLD A LIVE WASP IN YOUR MOUTH FOR 5 MINUTES?

Only female wasps can sting.

Tarantulas are the biggest kind of spider. They're often hairy, and they have two big fangs that they use to inject their prey with deadly venom.

WOULD YOU RATHER...

TRY TO COME DOWN FROM
THE TOP OF THE WORLD'S
TALLEST BUILDING ALL THE WAY
TO THE GROUND ON A NARROW SLIDE
THAT HAS NO RAILS ON THE SIDES

BY FLYING DOWN TO THE GROUND
IN A HUGE PAPER AIRPLANE
MADE BY AN EXPERT?

The world's tallest building is the
Taipei 101 in Taipei, Taiwan. It was
completed in 2004, has 101 stories,
and is 1,670 feet tall.

In 1998 Ken Blackburn set the world
record for the longest hand-launched
paper airplane flight. His plane flew
for a whopping 27.6 seconds.

WOULD YOU RATHER...

Always have peanut butter stuck to the roof of your mouth

OR

Always have gooey, melted marshmallows stuck to the roof of your mouth?

There's a word for the irrational fear of peanut butter sticking to the roof of your mouth: arachibutyrophobia.

In the United States more than 90 million pounds of marshmallows are eaten each year. They're used in everything from cakes to salads.

WOULD YOU RATHER...

Have to wear big, clunky glasses all **OR** day, every day for the rest of your life

Have one hand replaced by a hook like a pirate has?

All the presidents of the United States have worn glasses, but some of them didn't wear them in public.

In the original *Peter Pan* play, Captain Hook's right hand is a hook, but in Disney's movie *Peter Pan*, Captain Hook's left hand is a hook.

WOULD YOU RATHER...

ALWAYS HAVE TO DO ALL YOUR FAMILY'S LAUNDRY

OR

ALWAYS HAVE TO DO ALL YOUR FAMILY'S DISHES AFTER EVERY MEAL?

• The average family uses about 18,000 gallons of water every year just to do its laundry!

Knock-knock!
> Who's there?

Dishes.
> Dishes who?

Dishes the last question!